PRAISE FOR *SKETCHNOTES FOR EDUCATORS*

"I keep Sylvia Duckworth's sketchnotes around me as constant reminders of not only what I am supposed to do as a teacher but who I'm supposed to be. If a picture is worth a thousand words, a good sketchnote, like those in this book, are worth ten thousand. This book is a must buy for every teacher or person who wants to be inspired."

—Vicki A. Davis, author of *Reinventing Writing and Flattening Classrooms, Engaging Minds,* @coolcatteacher

"Sylvia Duckworth has an amazing way of simply and succinctly bringing ideas to life by illustrating concepts relevant to contemporary education. Her drawings cause educators to pause and reflect on how they can make meaningful changes in the best interest of their students. I personally have been a direct beneficiary of Sylvia's work, as she has interpreted many of my blog posts and quotes into drawings which I often share during speaking engagements. This book provides a one-stop place to find all of Sylvia's work; it is a goldmine for anyone interested in deeper discussions about education."

—George Couros, global educational consultant and author of *The Innovator's Mindset,* @georgecouros, georgecouros.ca

"Sylvia visually captures twenty-first-century teaching. Her sketchnotes make clear in a few page flips more than you could study in a year."

—Alice Keeler, author of *50 Things You Can Do with Google Classroom,* @alicekeeler, AliceKeeler.com

"I have been blessed enough to have seen my words and ideas come to life through the colors and images created by the talented Sylvia Duckworth.

"In this collection, Sylvia has not only found a creative way to express the best and most inspiring ideas in our community, but she has also found a way to validate and systematize a new language that will enable the conversation about education to reach an entirely new level."

—Angela Maiers, speaker, author, and founder of Choose2Matter, @angelamaiers, angelamaiers.com

"Rarely does a day go by where I don't see some impact of Sylvia's work, whether it's on social media, on a staff room wall in Hong Kong, Japan, or London, or it's being used in someone's presentation. Her impact has been truly global, and I would love to know exactly how many educators and, more importantly, children in their classrooms, have been helped or inspired by Sylvia and her work. This book is a fantastic place to dip into for inspiration or for help in different areas as an educator. Sylvia has an immeasurable skill; her sketches make complex processes and ideas come to life off the page and are made in such a way that everything becomes plain and simple. Read through, be inspired, and have a go at sketching, too. That's what she inspired me to do!"

—Mark Anderson, author of *Perfect ICT Every Lesson,* @ICTevangelist, ictevangelist.com

"This book embodies the power of visual learning—for both teachers and students—in a creative way that's rarely found in education books."

—Shelly Sanchez Terrell, international speaker and author of *The 30 Goals Challenge for Teachers*, @shellterrell, TeacherRebootCamp.com

"Whenever I hear the word sketchnote, Sylvia's work comes to mind. She is an artist with the ability to capture the big ideas from a talk, blog post, or discussion and showcase innovative educators from around the globe. Grab this book while you can!"

—Brian Aspinall, coding evangelist, @mraspinall, mraspinall.com

"When I began using Twitter five years ago, I was introduced to the beautiful and thought-provoking sketchnotes of Sylvia Duckworth. Many of the members of my PLN have remarked at how truly awesome her drawings are. They stand out in a Twitterverse that is crowded with a myriad of tweets and images. I knew that I had to ask Sylvia to create sketchnotes for a few of my most popular blog posts. Thankfully she did, and I am honored that they've been included in her new book. I highly recommend you pick up a copy!"

—Lee Araoz, district coordinator of instructional technology, @leearaoz, TheGoldenAgeofEducation.com

"I anxiously await each of Sylvia's new sketchnotes! She has the uncanny ability to listen or read carefully and pull out the important points in an educational article, a podcast, a TED Talk, or a lecture. Her sketchnotes also entice the audience to seek out the original article or video for viewing for further exploration and discussion."

—Kathy Schrock, educational technologist, @kathyschrock, schrockguide.net

"Sylvia Duckworth is the most generous educator and talented artist I am honored to know. I am lucky to have worked with her. I remember several late nights working with Sylvia over an idea around a few of our continuums. She persevered and came up with ideas that worked. The concepts for the continuums have made a huge impact in the education field, mainly because of the visuals Sylvia created. I so appreciate Sylvia and hope we collaborate on new designs in the future."

—Barbara Bray, creative learning strategist, co-founder of Personalize Learning, LLC, owner/founder, My eCoach and Rethinking Learning, and co-author of *Make Learning Personal* and *How to Personalize Learning*

"Sylvia has done a magical job of capturing the messages of countless educators by masterfully creating a series of sketchnotes that will no doubt inspire anyone with an interest in education. This sketchnote book is the first of its kind and surely deserves a spot in your professional library."

—Dr. Justin Tarte, @justintarte, justintarte.com

"Sylvia's sketchnotes reveal a little known truth about education that few others have been able to express in any medium—we live in the very best time to be an educator. As long as we continue to learn from those around us with an optimistic, open mind, there's nothing we can't change for the better."

—Kevin Brookhouser, author of
The 20time Project and Code in Every Class,
@brookhouser, kevinbrookhouser.com

"From her first sketchnotes shared with her professional learning network to the latest one retweeted hundreds of times, Sylvia Duckworth's drawings accurately outline pedagogical issues, mindsets, and challenges with simple and colourful elegance. They are the kind of image that makes forward-thinking educators say, 'That's just what I would have loved to draw and say!' Merci, Sylvia for the continued inspiration."

—Jacques Cool, director,
@zecool, CADRE21.org

"Sylvia has the ability to find issues that touch the hearts and emotions of educators and summarize them beautifully in sketches that capture the essence of the message simply and powerfully. This book is the essential collection of Sylvia's work. If you need quick inspiration, flip to any page, and you'll find it."

—Matt Miller, author of
Ditch That Textbook,
@jmattmiller, ditchthattextbook.com

Sketchnotes for Educators
© 2016 by Sylvia Duckworth

These books are available at special discounts when purchased in quantity for
use as premiums, promotions, fundraising, and educational use. For inquiries
and details, contact the publisher: edtechteam.com/press.
Published by EdTechTeam Press

Library of Congress Control Number: 2016956938
Paperback ISBN: 978-1-945167-23-2
eBook ISBN: 978-1-945167-24-9

Irvine, California

CONTENTS

✌ FOREWORD ✌

With apologies to *Star Trek*, or perhaps inspired by *Star Trek*, technology has allowed us "to go where no one has gone before."

The use of current technology has made us all better communicators. Who hasn't doodled to pass the time in class or in a meeting? Sylvia has taken this activity and combined it with the power of storytelling to create new and powerful ways to share messages. Sketchnotes are an engaging and powerful form of communication. It's the next frontier, and she has embraced it so nicely.

To date, Sylvia has used sketchnotes to extend the messages of others beyond the original post or presentation. It's not uncommon to see her works appear in blogs and articles by others, including my own. It provides a rich support and extension for those articles.

In this book, you'll have the opportunity to enjoy her work, and you'll be inspired to dig deeper into the original works, wonder what she'll sketch next, and perhaps even be pushed to learn how to create your own. No matter which direction this book takes you, you'll be all the better for it.

Doug Peterson

@dougpete
dougpete.wordpress.com

INTRODUCTION

I stopped drawing when I was around ten years old. I lost my love for art, as many kids do when they grow up. I did not believe I was a good artist, so what was the point?

Fast-forward forty-five years. In 2014, I started to notice some beautiful drawings related to education showing up on social media. People were taking notes from conferences and creating drawings in a doodling fashion. I learned it was called "sketchnoting," and I thought I would give it a try. I uploaded my first drawing to Flickr and Tweeted it out in January 2015. I never imagined in my wildest dreams that anyone would be interested in my drawings.

But educators were interested in my drawings, and before long, I was hooked on sketchnoting. I loved being able to express my ideas in a creative way, and the fact that my drawings seemed to resonate strongly with my PLN (Personal Learning Network) made me yearn to create more. I was on the constant hunt for interesting things to draw related to education: blog posts, graphics, articles, posters. Some ideas I borrowed from others; some ideas I came up with on my own.

With much surprise, I noticed that people were Tweeting photos of my drawings displayed on classroom and staffroom walls. The *Iceberg Illusion*, in particular, went viral, even appealing to people outside the educational community: entrepreneurs, athletes, coaches, writers, and managers. It thrilled me to know that my drawings were being shared and appreciated in so many ways.

This book is a collection of 100 of my most popular sketchnotes, which I have heard some people also refer to as edusketches since they often have to do with education. I created the book to provoke conversations about some of the topics covered, to entice readers to go to the original resource if referenced in the drawing, to provide links where the pieces can be downloaded, and to inspire readers to try sketchnoting themselves.

This book is *not* an instructional book on how to sketchnote. If you are interested in learning more, I invite you to look at a tutorial I created at bit.ly/sylsketchnote. Or, check out Mike Rohde's excellent resource: *The Sketchnote Handbook*. Karen Bosch is a teacher who created a very comprehensive iTunesU course called *Digital Sketchnotes for Visualizing Learning*. For sketchnoting with students, the best resource is Wendi Pillars' book *Visual Note-Taking for Educators: A Teacher's Guide to Student Creativity*. In case you're curious, I draw with the Procreate app on my iPad with the Musemee Notier Prime stylus, but there are many drawing apps and styluses to choose from. Of course, many people sketchnote with just a pen and paper.

Full disclaimer: I am not a traditional sketchnote artist because I do not sketchnote live. That is to say, I find it very difficult to sketchnote events in real time. Instead, I prefer to take notes during the event and then to draw afterward. Also, I often look for clipart and Creative Common licensed images on Google to help with my drawings. Sometimes, I will import a clipart directly into the canvas of my iPad and draw next to it, then delete the original image. Sometimes I just trace the clipart before deleting it. And now everyone knows one of the secrets to my sketchnoting!

I want to thank everyone from the bottom of my heart for the support I have had for my drawings. I am in constant awe of the brilliant teaching community around me. You are my inspiration.

Real Life

CHARACTER COUNTS

I saw a poster with the same words in my school library and I thought that it would make a great drawing because it is clear that one thing leads to another. The 6 Pillars of Character I found online and they rang true to me as well. If teachers and parents could successfully instill these six character traits in our children, what a different world it would be!

—SD

DOWNLOAD

bit.ly/sylsketch08

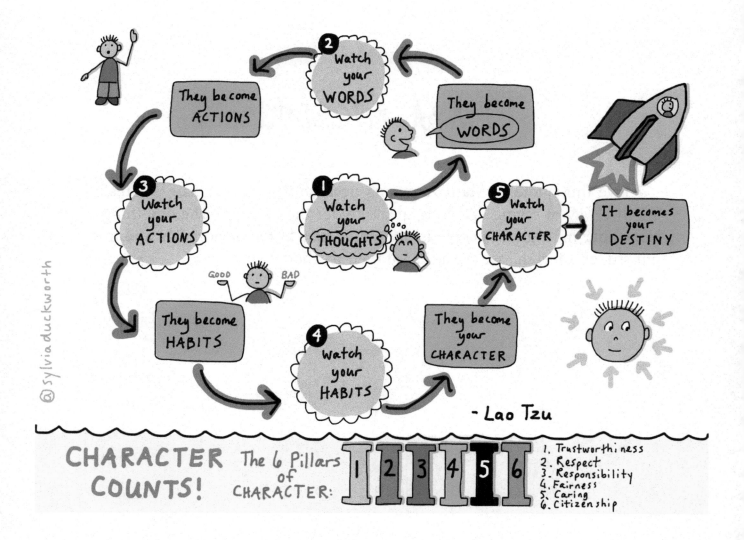

They become ACTIONS

② Watch your WORDS

They become WORDS

③ Watch your ACTIONS

① Watch your THOUGHTS

⑤ Watch your CHARACTER

It becomes your DESTINY

They become HABITS

GOOD BAD

④ Watch your HABITS

They become your CHARACTER

- Lao Tzu

CHARACTER COUNTS!

The 6 Pillars of CHARACTER:

1 2 3 4 5 6

1. Trustworthiness
2. Respect
3. Responsibility
4. Fairness
5. Caring
6. Citizenship

MAYA ANGELOU

I love this quote of Maya Angelou's because it is just so true. It's really another way of saying, "Actions speak louder than words." The one thing I remember most about people is, were they nice to me or not? I'm sure that our students feel the same way about their teachers.

—SD

DOWNLOAD
bit.ly/sylsketch11

People will forget what you said,

People will forget what you did,

But people will never forget how you made them feel. — Maya Angelou

@sylviaduckworth

17

MANAGING COMPLEX CHANGE

I saw this graphic on Twitter and was intrigued by it. It struck me as being applicable to many kinds of organizations, including schools. (I'm not sure about the "Incentives" category for schools, unless they are intrinsic incentives.)

—SD

DOWNLOAD
bit.ly/sylsketch18

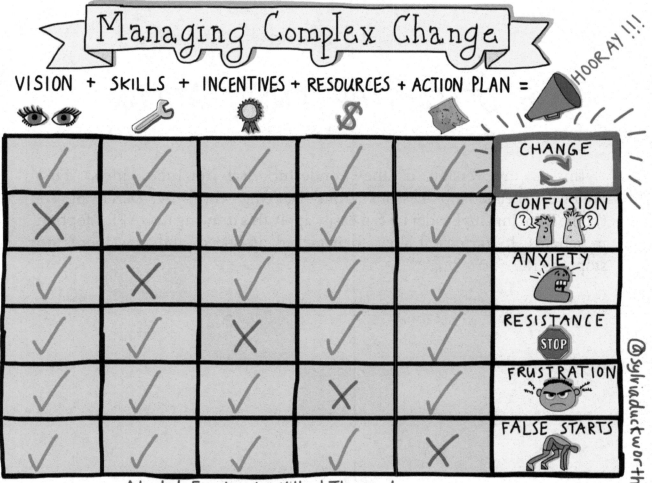

Managing Complex Change

VISION + SKILLS + INCENTIVES + RESOURCES + ACTION PLAN = HOORAY!!!

✓	✓	✓	✓	✓	CHANGE
✗	✓	✓	✓	✓	CONFUSION
✓	✗	✓	✓	✓	ANXIETY
✓	✓	✗	✓	✓	RESISTANCE
✓	✓	✓	✗	✓	FRUSTRATION
✓	✓	✓	✓	✗	FALSE STARTS

Adapted from Knoster, Villa, & Thousand

@sylviaduckworth

5 STAGES OF INNOVATION

This is my version of the wonderful viral YouTube video, "First Follower: Leadership Lessons from Dancing Guy" by Derek Silvers (bit.ly/DancingGuyLeader). I can easily apply this drawing to GAFE adoption in schools. It started off slow, then picked up speed, and now there's no stopping it.

—SD

DOWNLOAD
bit.ly/sylsketch19

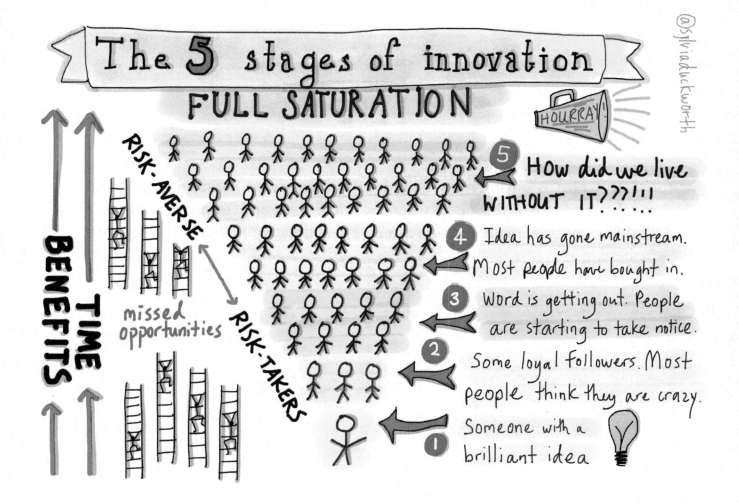

The 5 stages of innovation
FULL SATURATION

@sylviaduckworth

HOURRAY!

5 How did we live WITHOUT IT???!!!

4 Idea has gone mainstream. Most people have bought in.

3 Word is getting out. People are starting to take notice.

2 Some loyal followers. Most people think they are crazy.

1 Someone with a brilliant idea

RISK-AVERSE

RISK-TAKERS

missed opportunities

BENEFITS

TIME

LIFE

L.R. Knost is an internationally best-selling, award-winning author and speaker, and I loved this poem when I saw it on Twitter. We have to remember that life can be a challenge sometimes, but ultimately, we are all so lucky to be here.

—SD

DOWNLOAD
bit.ly/sylsketch25

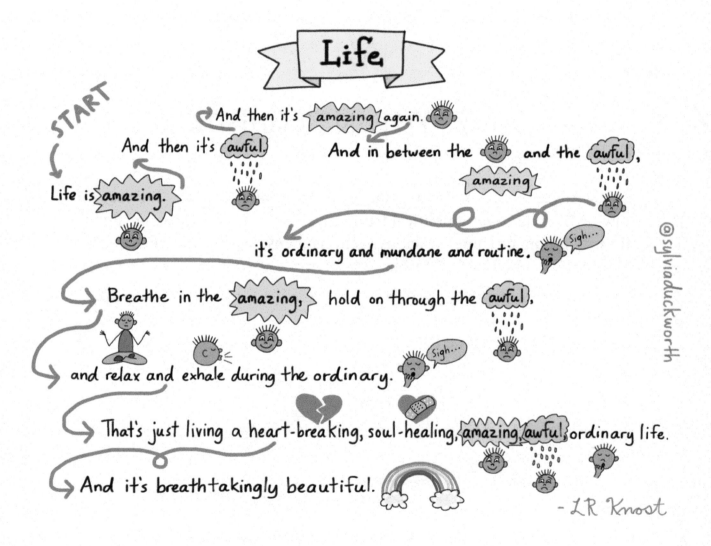

@sylviaduckworth

23

LOVE THY NEIGHBOR

I saw these words on Twitter one day, and went "Right on." I Tweet this drawing out whenever a political figure says something disparaging about a minority group, or some atrocious event happens, like the horrific shooting of gay patrons in Orlando, Florida.

—SD

DOWNLOAD
bit.ly/sylsketch26

Love Thy Neighbour

Thy white neighbour
Thy black neighbour
Thy Christian neighbour
Thy homeless neighbour
Thy addicted neighbour
Thy gay neighbour
Thy Hindu neighbour
Thy Muslim neighbour
Thy First Nations neighbour
Thy Asian neighbour
Thy atheist neighbour
Thy Jewish neighbour

@sylviaduckworth

Author unknown

THE LITTLE PRINCE

I made this drawing because I fell in love with the novel, *The Little Prince*, in my grade-13 French class. Its magical quality and insightfulness made a lasting impression on me. These are some of my favourite quotes from the book.

—SD

DOWNLOAD
bit.ly/sylsketch34

The Little Prince

It is the time you have wasted for your rose that makes your rose so important.

My planet is so small. I need a sheep. Draw me a sheep.

You - only you - will have stars that can laugh.

@sylviaduckworth

It is only with the heart that one can see rightly; what is essential is invisible to the eye.

If you tame me, then we shall need eachother. To me, you will be unique in all the world. To you, I shall be unique in all the world.

Grown-ups never understand anything by themselves and it is tiresome for children to be always and forever explaining things to them.

10 THINGS THAT WILL HAPPEN IF YOU STEP OUT OF YOUR COMFORT ZONE

"I decided to write this blog post as more and more amazing things started happening in my life when I decided to get out of my comfort zone. Challenging your mind's natural tendency to stay comfortable is something that I believe is required in order for you to finish your day comfortable and get a regret-free sleep at night."

—Oskar Nowik

@oskarnowik
growthzer.com

DOWNLOAD
bit.ly/sylsketch35

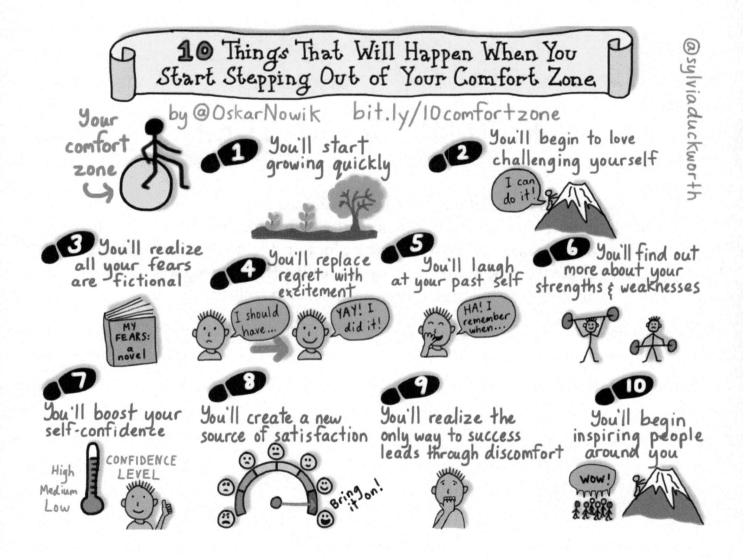

ANATOMY OF AN IDEA

This happens to me often: After I share an idea in my community or on social media, it often comes back to me better than before as other people run with it and try it out. I believe this is why educators love to share so much: It's exciting to see the genesis from an idea to a reality. This drawing was inspired by Colleen Rose's (@ColleenKR) drawing here: bit.ly/colleenkr.

—SD

DOWNLOAD
bit.ly/sylsketch37

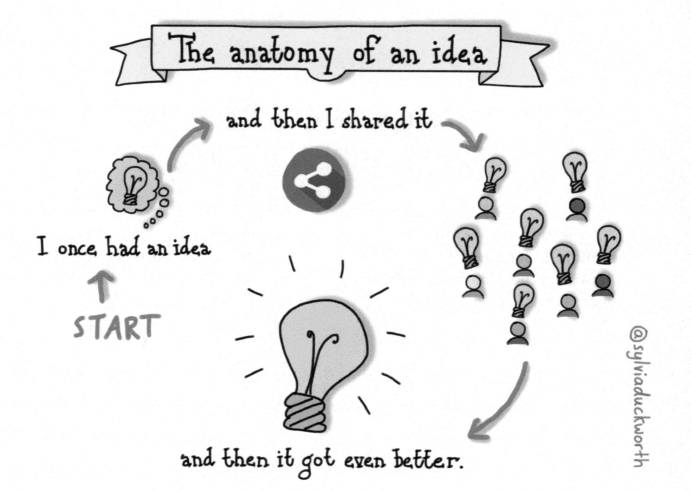

The anatomy of an idea

and then I shared it

I once had an idea

START

and then it got even better.

@sylviaduckworth

10 THINGS WE CAN LEARN FROM SUPERHEROES

I saw this blog post on Twitter: "6 Things We Can Learn from Superheroes" by Julia Lepetit and Tristan Cooper, and I thought it would make a great drawing. I took some of the ideas from the post and added some more. Who doesn't love a superhero?

—SD

DOWNLOAD

bit.ly/sylsketch40

10 Things We Can Learn from Superheroes

1. We all have something we are good at.

2. Being different can give you power.

3. Embrace who you are and be proud of it.

4. Adversity can be overcome.

5. True strength is helping others find their own.

6. Facing danger is the best way to overcome your fears.

7. Not everyone needs rescuing.

8. Nice guys don't always finish last.

9. You don't need superpowers to be a hero.

10. If you want to change the world, start with yourself.

@sylviaduckworth

MODES OF THINKING

I once did a talk on creativity and creative thinking, and while doing my research I got very confused about the terminology for different modes of thinking. I thought that a drawing would clarify the different terms. As teachers we need to develop our students' divergent and convergent thinking skills to allow them to think laterally, or "outside the box," in order to be good problem solvers and innovators.

—SD

DOWNLOAD
bit.ly/sylsketch41

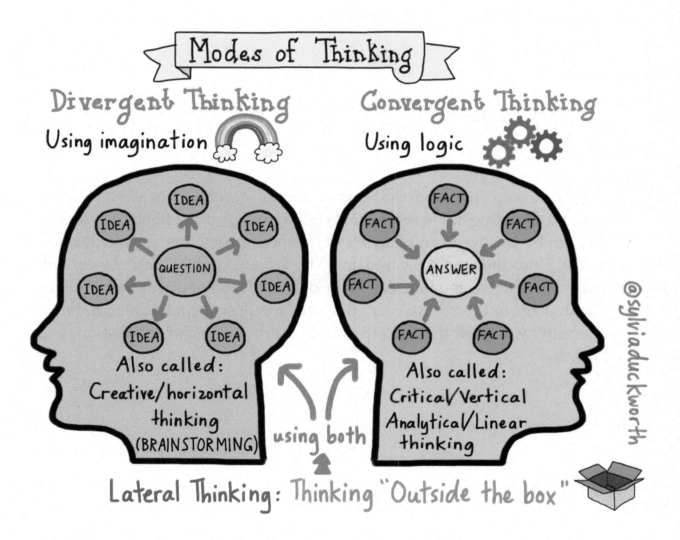

12 BENEFITS OF CREATIVITY

This drawing came from the heart as I basically just thought about all of the ways sketchnoting has benefitted me since I took it up as a hobby. Obviously, you can be creative in so many ways; it is not restricted to any one form of media. I also thought of my husband who loves to cook because it gives him a creative outlet after a long day in the office. It is so important that we allow our students to be creative every day and to expose them to different forms of creativity to allow them to tap into their perhaps unrealized passions and talents.

—SD

DOWNLOAD
bit.ly/sylsketch45

12 Benefits of Creativity

CREATIVITY

1. Creativity is multi-disciplinary

2. Creativity allows you to express yourself

3. Creativity promotes thinking outside the box and problem-solving

4. Creativity reduces stress and anxiety

5. Creativity allows you to enter your 😊 and have fun! HAPPY ZONE

6. Creativity gives you a sense of purpose

7. Creativity leads to feelings of accomplishment and pride

8. Creativity can link you to others with the same passion

9. Creativity improves your ability to focus

10. Creativity promotes risk-taking & iteration

11. Creativity is a pre-requisite for innovation

12. Creativity encourages us to be life-long learners

"Creativity now is as important in education as literacy and we should treat it with the same status."
-Ken Robinson

@sylviaduckworth

10 REASONS WHY FAILURE IS IMPORTANT

It's a bit of a cliché to educators when they hear that failure is important. I thought that this drawing might come in handy if anyone were to ever ask, "Exactly why is failure important?" The most critical element of failure, however, is the notion of having to try again. Because only then will you truly learn from your mistakes.

—SD

DOWNLOAD
bit.ly/sylsketch48

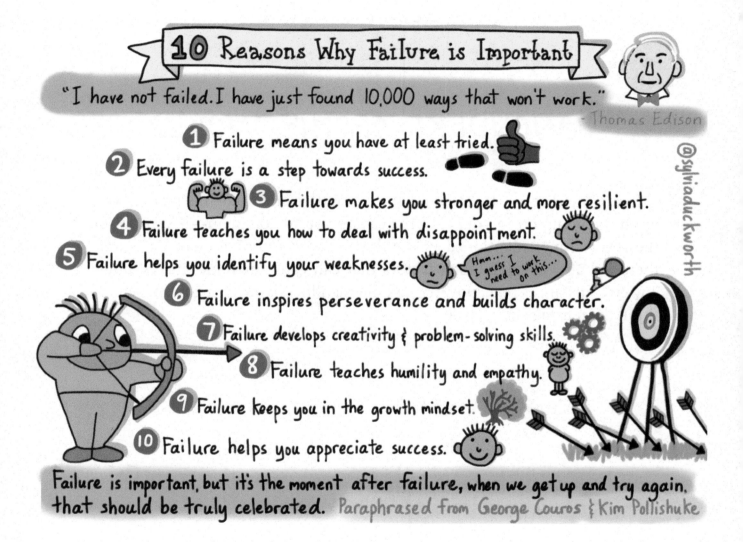

10 Reasons Why Failure is Important

"I have not failed. I have just found 10,000 ways that won't work."
— Thomas Edison

1. Failure means you have at least tried.
2. Every failure is a step towards success.
3. Failure makes you stronger and more resilient.
4. Failure teaches you how to deal with disappointment.
5. Failure helps you identify your weaknesses.

Hmm... I guess I need to work on this...

6. Failure inspires perseverance and builds character.
7. Failure develops creativity & problem-solving skills.
8. Failure teaches humility and empathy.
9. Failure keeps you in the growth mindset.
10. Failure helps you appreciate success.

Failure is important, but it's the moment after failure, when we get up and try again, that should be truly celebrated. Paraphrased from George Couros & Kim Pollishuke

@sylviaduckworth

7 WONDERS OF THE WORLD

I saw this list on Twitter and it occurred to me that—no matter what might be going on in your life that causes you to complain—if you can do the seven things mentioned in the drawing, you're doing okay. Of course, there are always extenuating factors that can cause extreme misery under any circumstances (e.g., poverty and mental illness), but in a general sense, I think the message holds true.

—SD

DOWNLOAD
bit.ly/sylsketch52

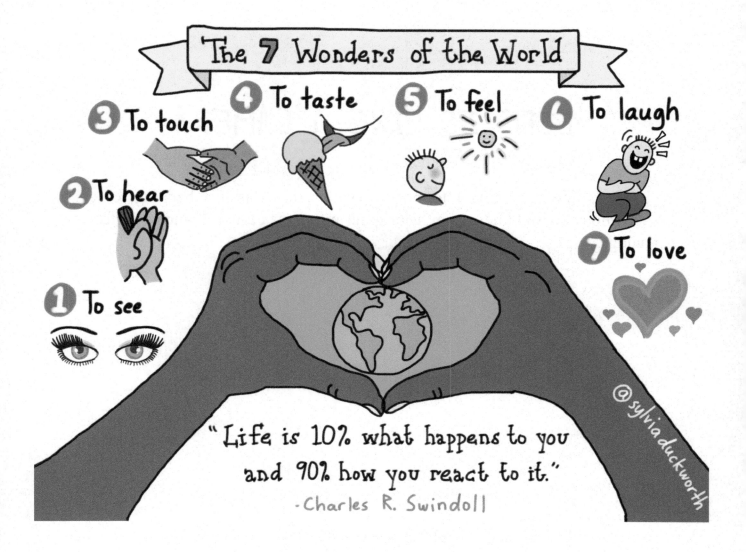

LIFE IS LIKE A CAMERA

This is another quote I found on Twitter that was just begging for a sketchnote. I wish I knew who the original author is because it's such a perfect analogy.

—SD

DOWNLOAD
bit.ly/sylsketch53

Life is like a camera...

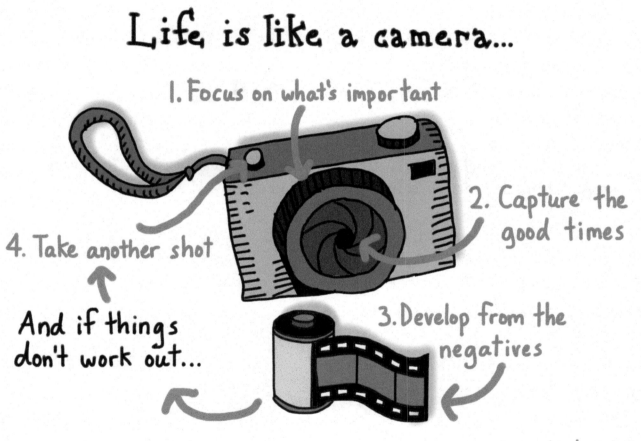

1. Focus on what's important

2. Capture the good times

3. Develop from the negatives

4. Take another shot

And if things don't work out...

@sylviaduckworth

CREATIVE PEOPLE

I saw this original list on Twitter and went, "Yes. Yes. Yes. Yes…" to every point. I think that many creative people would agree!

—SD

DOWNLOAD

bit.ly/sylsketch64

Hate the rules

RULES

Think with their heart

Are easily bored

Colour outside the lines

Change their mind a lot

Creative People

Make lots of mistakes

OOPS!

Dream big

Are risk takers

Work independently

Have a reputation for eccentricity

@sylviaduckworth

45

ALL I REALLY NEED TO KNOW
I LEARNED IN KINDERGARTEN

Twenty-five years ago, Robert Fulghum published this simple credo, and it will never grow old. If you Google the title of this drawing, you will find a multitude of different representations of this poem. I thought it was time for a sketchnoted version.

—SD

DOWNLOAD
bit.ly/sylsketch72

All I Really Need To Know I Learned in Kindergarten

By Robert Fulgham

1. Share everything
2. Play fair
3. Don't hit people
4. Put things back where you found them.
5. Klean up your own mess.
6. Don't take things that aren't yours
7. Say u r sorry when u hurt someone
8. Wash your hands before u eat
9. Flush
10. Warm cookies and cold milk are good for you
11. Live a balanced life: learn. Think. Draw. Paint. Sing. Dance. Play. Work.
12. Take a nap every afternoon.
13. Be aware of wonder
14. Look around
15. When you go out into the world, watch for traffic, hold hands, & stick 2gether.

@sylviaduckworth

THE ICEBERG ILLUSION

"The Iceberg Illusion depicts so clearly what we so often miss when we witness success. We see the performance: the brilliant free-kick, or the wonderful painting, or whatever. What we don't see is the hours of practice, the support, the brilliant coaching and teaching. Understanding these hidden elements is crucial to instilling growth mindset. It is why this illustration is so powerful."

—Matthew Syed

@matthewsyed
matthewsyed.co.uk

DOWNLOAD
bit.ly/sylsketch68

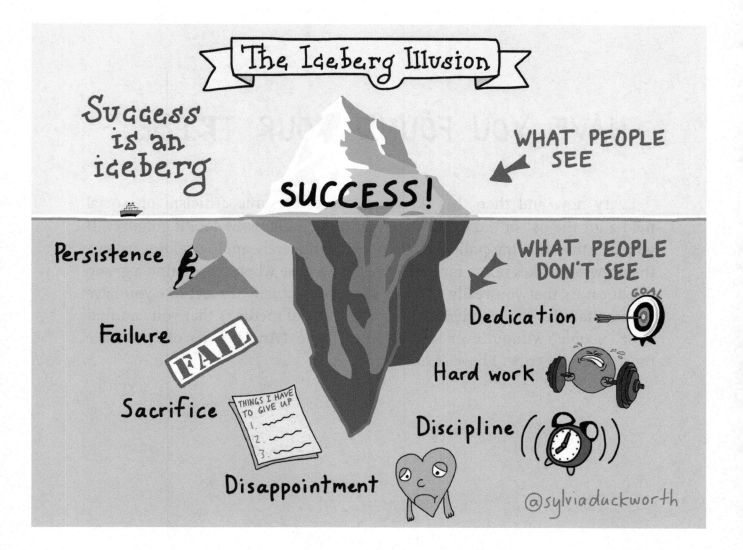

49

HAVE YOU FOUND YOUR TRIBE?

Every now and then this sketchnote receives some criticism on social media for the use of the word "Tribe" and the indigenous-looking figures. If you find this drawing politically incorrect, I sincerely apologize. Regardless, the drawing strikes home for many people because when you do find a group of educators that you really connect with, you actually do feel like you have found a family. The wonderful thing about social media is that you can find your "people" without ever leaving your house. (And yes, it's okay to have more than one tribe. I have several.)

—SD

DOWNLOAD
bit.ly/sylsketch69

Have You Found Your Tribe?

You know that you have found your tribe when...

1. You are inspired and energized by them.
2. You feel that your ideas and opinions matter.
3. You are motivated to share with them.
4. You feel accepted and appreciated.
5. You feel nourished from the outside and from the inside.
6. You can turn to them for help at any time.
7. They advise you without judgement.
8. You share similar passions and beliefs.
9. You are on the same wavelength.
10. Life just wouldn't be the same without them.

@sylviaduckworth

WHERE THE MAGIC HAPPENS

This is one of my earliest sketchnotes and one of my favourites. I can so relate to the message. Every time I step out of my comfort zone, the zone gets wider and wider. There's nothing sadder than to see the wasted potential of someone who is too afraid to try new things. The bottom line is, how can we ask our students to step out of their comfort zones if we don't model this ourselves?

—SD

DOWNLOAD
bit.ly/sylsketch78

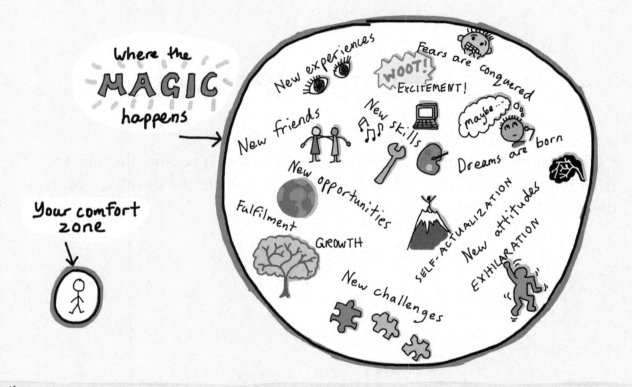

"You gain strength, courage and confidence by every experience in which you really stop to look fear in the face... You must do the thing you think you cannot do." · Eleanor Roosevelt

10 STEPS TO HAPPINESS

This was another quote I first saw on Twitter. I love it because the message is so important: The key to happiness is to accentuate the positive, not to dwell on the negative.

—SD

DOWNLOAD
bit.ly/sylsketch84

10 Steps to Happiness

1. Hate less, love more
2. Worry less, dance more
3. Take less, give more
4. Consume less, create more
5. Frown less, smile more
6. Talk less, listen more
7. Fear less, try more
8. Judge less, accept more
9. Watch less, do more
10. Complain less, appreciate more

@sylvia duckworth

WHAT WE REMEMBER

There are so many different versions of this idea online that it is impossible to find the original source. It is also controversial, as many people have pointed out to me that these figures are not based on actual fact. It reminds me of the Benjamin Franklin quote, "Tell me and I forget. Teach me and I may remember. Involve me and I learn." In any case, the point is that giving students hands-on, active experiences as opposed to lecture-style, passive experiences is always more meaningful and beneficial.

—SD

DOWNLOAD
bit.ly/sylsketch89

What We Remember

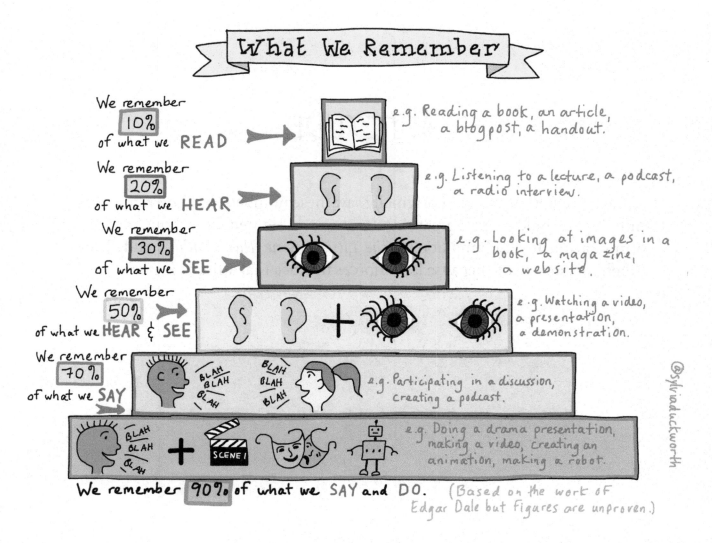

We remember 10% of what we READ — e.g. Reading a book, an article, a blogpost, a handout.

We remember 20% of what we HEAR — e.g. Listening to a lecture, a podcast, a radio interview.

We remember 30% of what we SEE — e.g. Looking at images in a book, a magazine, a website.

We remember 50% of what we HEAR & SEE — e.g. Watching a video, a presentation, a demonstration.

We remember 70% of what we SAY — e.g. Participating in a discussion, creating a podcast.

We remember 90% of what we SAY and DO. — e.g. Doing a drama presentation, making a video, creating an animation, making a robot.

(Based on the work of Edgar Dale but figures are unproven.)

@sylviaduckworth

ATTITUDE

I don't remember where I originally saw these numbers, but I do remember thinking it would make a great sketchnote, and I immediately thought of one of my favourite children's books, *The Little Engine That Could*. I added the Ralph Marston quote because it reinforces the idea that attitude is everything.

—SD

DOWNLOAD

bit.ly/sylsketch91

ATTITUDE

RATE OF SUCCESS

100% · I can.
90% · I know I can.
80% · I will.
70% · I think I can.
60% · I'll try.
50% · I think I might.
40% · I want to.
30% · I wish I could.
20% · I don't know how.
10% · I can't.
0% · I won't.

"Excellence is not a skill.
It is an attitude."
- Ralph Marston

@ sylviaduckworth

59

WHISPERED THE HEART

I first saw this quote on Twitter, but the original author is unknown. I love it because it is a mantra that I live by: Sometimes you just have to follow your heart no matter how many other voices are telling you not to. Because only then will you find meaningfulness and true happiness.

—SD

DOWNLOAD

bit.ly/sylsketch94

THE ONLY PERSON

I love this quote from Rushton Hurley (@rushtonh, nextvista.org) because it's so easy to fall into the trap of comparing yourself with other people whom you deem to have more expertise in a certain area. This is particularly relevant to teachers learning about technology.

—SD

DOWNLOAD
bit.ly/sylsketch95

The only person you need to
compare yourself with is who
you were yesterday.

-Rushton
Hurley

Yesterday   Today   Tomorrow

THE LOTTERY OF LIFE

    I saw this quote by Collective-Evolution.com and I was struck by its simple and important message. It's easy to judge people for things over which they have no control, yet we do it all the time. We have a responsibility as educators to constantly remind our students how wrong this is and we need to model and embody non-discriminatory behavior ourselves at all times.

—SD

DOWNLOAD

bit.ly/sylsketch98

In the lottery of life, there are things that people <u>do not</u> control:

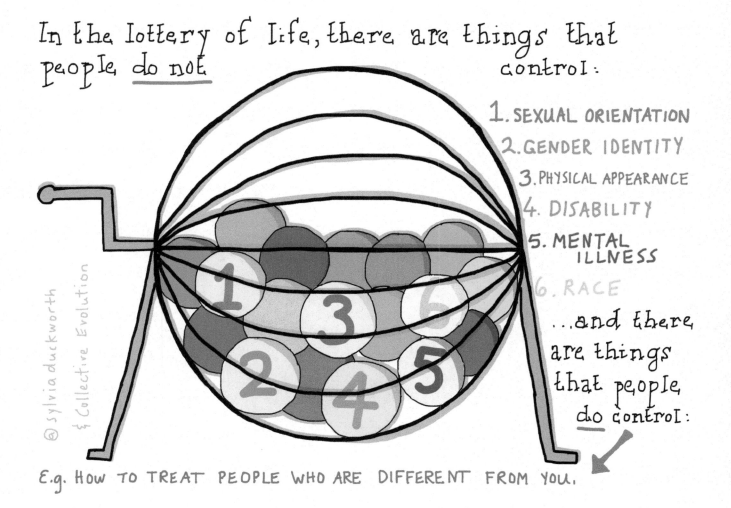

1. SEXUAL ORIENTATION
2. GENDER IDENTITY
3. PHYSICAL APPEARANCE
4. DISABILITY
5. MENTAL ILLNESS
6. RACE

...and there are things that people <u>do</u> control:

E.g. HOW TO TREAT PEOPLE WHO ARE DIFFERENT FROM YOU.

@ sylvia duckworth
& Collective Evolution

Real Education

THE 6 Cs OF EDUCATION

Michael Fullan is a Canadian educational researcher and former dean of the Ontario Institute for Studies in Education (OISE). He came up with the idea of the 6 Cs—the competencies our students must achieve throughout their education to become successful in life and in society.

—SD

DOWNLOAD

bit.ly/sylsketch02

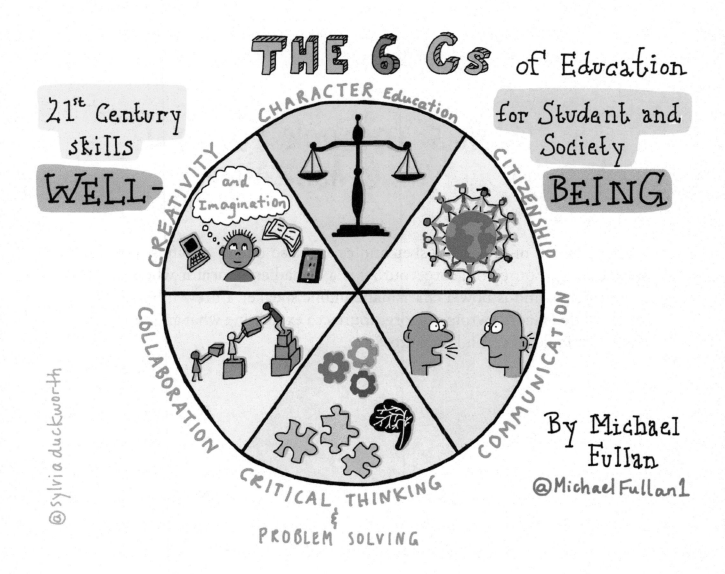

THE 6 Cs of Education for Student and Society

21st Century skills WELL-BEING

CHARACTER Education

CREATIVITY (and Imagination)

CITIZENSHIP

COLLABORATION

CRITICAL THINKING & PROBLEM SOLVING

COMMUNICATION

By Michael Fullan @MichaelFullan1

@sylviaduckworth

69

8 THINGS TO LOOK FOR IN TODAY'S CLASSROOM

This was one of my earlier sketchnotes and also one of my most popular ones. George Couros (@georgecouros) is a Canadian educator who used to be a principal and is now a charismatic public speaker. I drew it based on a blog post that George wrote at georgecouros.ca explaining what an innovative classroom looks like. (bit.ly/gcouros8)

—SD

DOWNLOAD

bit.ly/sylsketch03

8 Things to Look for in Today's Classroom
by George Couros

1 VOICE
★ Students should learn from others and then share their learning.

2 CHOICE
★ STRENGTH-BASED LEARNING
★ Give students a choice.

3 TIME FOR REFLECTION
★ EVERYONE (teachers, admin, students) should write and reflect on what is being learned.

8 CONNECTED LEARNING
★ Bring experts into your class via social media and video-conferencing.

CLASSROOMS need to be LEARNER-FOCUSSED

4 OPPORTUNITIES for INNOVATION
★ Example: Build a hovercraft from a YouTube video!
(yes, it can be done!)

7 SELF-ASSESSMENT
★ Important that students know how to do this.
★ Use portfolios.

6 PROBLEM SOLVERS/FINDERS
★ Give students tough challenges and let them find innovative solutions.

5 CRITICAL THINKERS
★ Ask questions and challenge what you see.

BLAH BLAH BLAH

bit.ly/gcouros8

@sylviaduckworth

71

GROWTH MINDSET VS
FIXED MINDSET

I saw a version of this on Twitter and decided to re-draw it, thinking that a tree would be a good representation of a growth mindset, while a brick wall would represent a fixed mindset. It's easy to see how a growth mindset will lead to success, while a fixed mindset will only lead to frustration. I suspect that Carol Dweck's work on growth mindset and Angela Duckworth's work on grit have a lot to do with the original infographic I saw by Reid Wilson.

—SD

DOWNLOAD
bit.ly/sylsketch04

Growth mindset vs fixed mindset

SUCCESS ⟷ FRUSTRATION

Growth mindset	Fixed mindset
1. I can learn anything I want to.	1. I'm either good at it, or I'm not.
2. When I'm frustrated, I persevere.	2. When I'm frustrated, I give up.
3. I like to challenge myself.	3. I don't like to be challenged.
4. When I fail, I learn.	4. When I fail, I'm no good.
5. I like being told that I try hard.	5. I like being told that I'm smart.
6. If my classmates succeed, I'm inspired.	6. If my classmates succeed, I feel threatened.
7. My effort and attitude determine everything.	7. My abilities determine everything.

GRIT ⟷ Learned helplessness

From Reid Wilson
@wayfarepath

@sylviaduckworth

73

'I HAVE A DREAM'

"I was frustrated with the standardized testing mandates from the New Jersey Department of Education after learning that, for the three months of PARCC testing in 2015, my district was shutting down all student access to technology. So I published a blog post on Dr. Martin Luther King, Jr. Day. Inspired by Dr. King's vision and iconic 'I Have a Dream' speech, I wrote about my dreams for education."

—Kate Baker

@ktbkr4

kbakerbyodlit.blogspot.ca

DOWNLOAD

bit.ly/sylsketch05

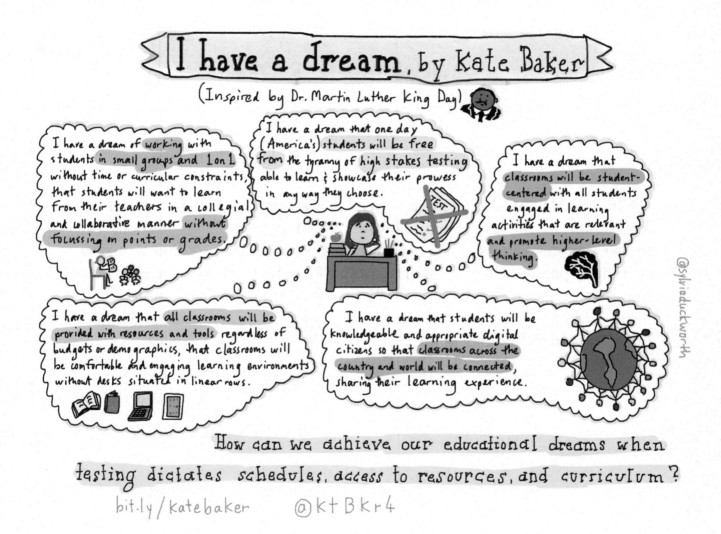

I have a dream, by Kate Baker

(Inspired by Dr. Martin Luther King Day)

I have a dream of working with students in small groups and 1 on 1 without time or curricular constraints, that students will want to learn from their teachers in a collegial and collaborative manner without focussing on points or grades.

I have a dream that one day (America's) students will be free from the tyranny of high stakes testing able to learn & showcase their prowess in any way they choose.

I have a dream that classrooms will be student-centered with all students engaged in learning activities that are relevant and promote higher-level thinking.

I have a dream that all classrooms will be provided with resources and tools regardless of budgets or demographics, that classrooms will be comfortable and engaging learning environments without desks situated in linear rows.

I have a dream that students will be knowledgeable and appropriate digital citizens so that classrooms across the country and world will be connected, sharing their learning experience.

How can we achieve our educational dreams when testing dictates schedules, access to resources, and curriculum?

bit.ly/katebaker   @ktBkr4

@sylviaduckworth

75

SAMR

"The SAMR Model is a very helpful way of looking at technology integration in the classroom; however, most depictions of it focus on the written descriptors. Sylvia and I discussed how SAMR could be like a swimming pool in which users move from the shallow end to the deep end as they gain confidence in using tech. This evolved into an ocean, and the end result is a beautiful graphic that educators can use to critically reflect on their integration of technology in the classroom."

—Peter Maxwell

@edappadvice

DOWNLOAD
bit.ly/sylsketch36

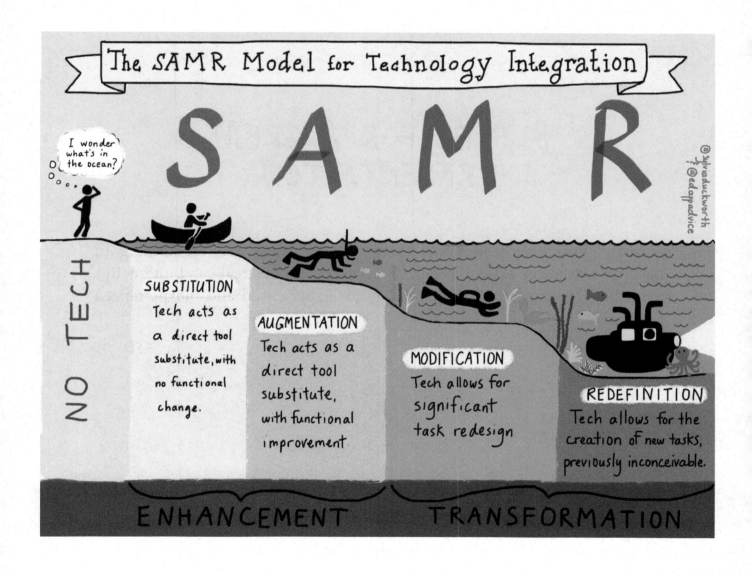

8 TIPS FOR A GREAT PRESENTATION

Many presenters who know their content really well are lacking in basic presentation skills. "Death by PowerPoint" is real, and these tips from EdTechTeam are great reminders for experienced and inexperienced presenters.

—SD

DOWNLOAD
bit.ly/sylsketch42

8 Tips for a Great Presentation

By @EdTechTeam

1 Plan to go slower than you think! Content that seems easy to you may be difficult for your audience to follow.

2 Share what you're passionate about. People can tell if you're not super excited about what you're sharing.

3 Have your attendees gotten a chance to PLAY or MAKE? Make sure they do!

Hey, look what I can do!

4 Play music, walk around and chat with people, or play a game to engage the room between sessions.

5 Don't get so wrapped up in delivering content that you forget about the human beings in the room.

zzz... zzz... zzz...

BLAH BLAH BLAH

6 Use a slide deck as your outline, but make sure you present your topic "live" and have the participants play along with you!

What do you think?

7 Be better than a Hangout. Make the session interactive. What will make the in-the-room experience unique?

WOW! That's SO cool!

8 Provide time for your attendees to synthesize what they have learned in your session.

@sylviaduckworth

CONTINUUM OF VOICE

"In our post, 'Learner Voice Demonstrates Commitment to Building Agency,' we adapted the Continuum of Voice chart from the research from Toshalis and Nakkula at the Students at the Center. Voice gives learners a chance to share their opinions about something they believe in. We added examples that illustrate each level to support implementation at each level in more detail in another post."

—Barbara Bray

@bbray27

and Kathleen McClaskey

@khmmc
Personalize Learning, LLC

DOWNLOAD
bit.ly/sylsketch44

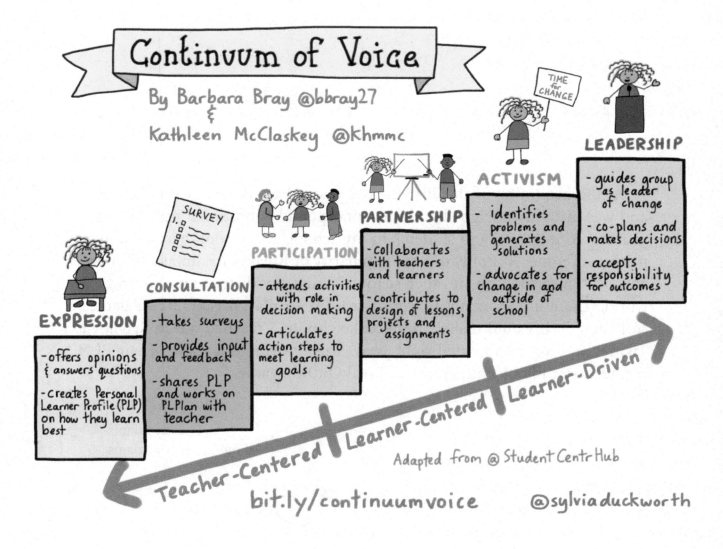

Continuum of Voice

By Barbara Bray @bbray27
&
Kathleen McClaskey @khmmc

EXPRESSION
- offers opinions & answers questions
- creates Personal Learner Profile (PLP) on how they learn best

CONSULTATION
- takes surveys
- provides input and feedback
- shares PLP and works on PLPlan with teacher

PARTICIPATION
- attends activities with role in decision making
- articulates action steps to meet learning goals

PARTNERSHIP
- collaborates with teachers and learners
- contributes to design of lessons, projects and assignments

ACTIVISM
- identifies problems and generates solutions
- advocates for change in and outside of school

LEADERSHIP
- guides group as leader of change
- co-plans and makes decisions
- accepts responsibility for outcomes

TIME for CHANGE

Teacher-Centered | Learner-Centered | Learner-Driven

Adapted from @ Student Centr Hub

bit.ly/continuumvoice   @sylviaduckworth

10 REASONS TO PLAY BreakOutEdu

"At the beginning of the 2015 school year, I learned about BreakOutEdu and was instantly intrigued with the concept and educational possibilities. I introduced it to staff and students in my school, and it soon became a huge passion of mine. Not only did the popularity of BreakOutEdu take off in my school, it also took off in other schools across my district and around the world. There are so many powerful reasons to play BreakOutEdu games, so I thought it would make a perfect sketchnote. I reached out to Sylvia via Twitter and we collaborated right away. This drawing is a result of our PLN connection and our mutual love of BreakOutEdu games."

—Maria Galanis

@mariagalanis
about.me/mariagalanis

DOWNLOAD
bit.ly/sylsketch47

10 Reasons to Play BreakOutEdu

By @MariaGalanis   @sylviaduckworth

1. It's fun for everyone!
   I LOVE THIS! ME TOO! ME THREE!

2. It is adaptable to any subject area
   MATH SOCIAL STUDIES SCIENCE PHYS ED MUSIC LANGUAGE ARTS DRAMA VISUAL ARTS

3. It promotes collaboration and team-building

4. It develops problem-solving & critical thinking skills

5. It enhances communication skills

6. It challenges players to persevere

7. It builds inference skills
   IF THIS... THEN THAT

8. Students learn to work under pressure
   BREAKOUT 00:45:00

9. It's student-centered

10. It's inquiry-based learning at its best
    THINKING CAP

83

TECHNOLOGY WILL NEVER REPLACE TEACHERS

"Technology is abundant, everywhere, and talked about all of the time. That being said, it will never replace great teachers. The best teachers do, however, use almost anything they can to create opportunities for all the students they serve. This still focuses on great teaching and learning, but the technological opportunities that are available to teachers now can be truly transformational for our learners."

—George Couros

@georgecouros
georgecouros.ca

DOWNLOAD
bit.ly/sylsketch57

Technology will never replace great teachers,

But technology in the hands of a great teacher can be transformational. *George Couros*

85

IN THE REAL WORLD

"Sometimes the phrase 'in the real world' is thrown around to justify a classroom policy or assignment. If our classes were truly mimicking the real world, students would not be raising their hand to go to the bathroom, and they could use their cell phone anytime to do a Google search for information."

—Alice Keeler

@alicekeeler
AliceKeeler.com

DOWNLOAD
bit.ly/sylsketch59

10 TECHNOLOGY RULES

Jessica Sanders from Whooosreading.org asked me to draw this sketchnote. I think the ten rules are good for young tech users, and I would recommend printing and displaying this drawing near devices in your classroom.

—SD

DOWNLOAD
bit.ly/sylsketch61

11 TIPS FOR KEEPING UP WITH TECHNOLOGY

Sitting at home one day, I started to notice my Twitter feed being bombarded with #ISTE tweets. ISTE is the biggest EdTech conference in North America, and as I started to click on the resources that teachers were sharing, I began to feel overwhelmed. Oh my goodness, how can I keep up with all of this? I thought. So I created this sketchnote to help teachers who feel the same way towards technology from time to time.

—SD

DOWNLOAD
bit.ly/sylsketch67

11 Tips for Keeping Up With Technology

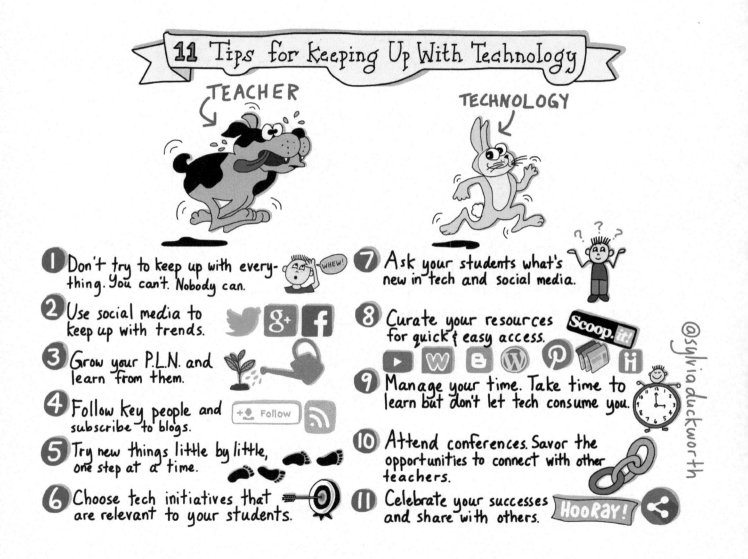

TEACHER

TECHNOLOGY

1. Don't try to keep up with everything. You can't. Nobody can. WHEW!

2. Use social media to keep up with trends.

3. Grow your P.L.N. and learn from them.

4. Follow key people and subscribe to blogs. +Follow

5. Try new things little by little, one step at a time.

6. Choose tech initiatives that are relevant to your students.

7. Ask your students what's new in tech and social media.

8. Curate your resources for quick & easy access. Scoop.it!

9. Manage your time. Take time to learn but don't let tech consume you.

10. Attend conferences. Savor the opportunities to connect with other teachers.

11. Celebrate your successes and share with others. HOORAY!

@sylviaduckworth

91

9 CHARACTERISTICS OF INNOVATIVE LEADERS

This was another blog post that I read that just demanded a sketchnote. It's a good exercise to read the points and determine where your school leader shines and where he or she needs improvement. If most of them check "No," it's probably time for you to move on.

—SD

DOWNLOAD
bit.ly/sylsketch77

9 Characteristics of Innovative Leaders

By Jack Zenger @jhzenger bit.ly/9leaders

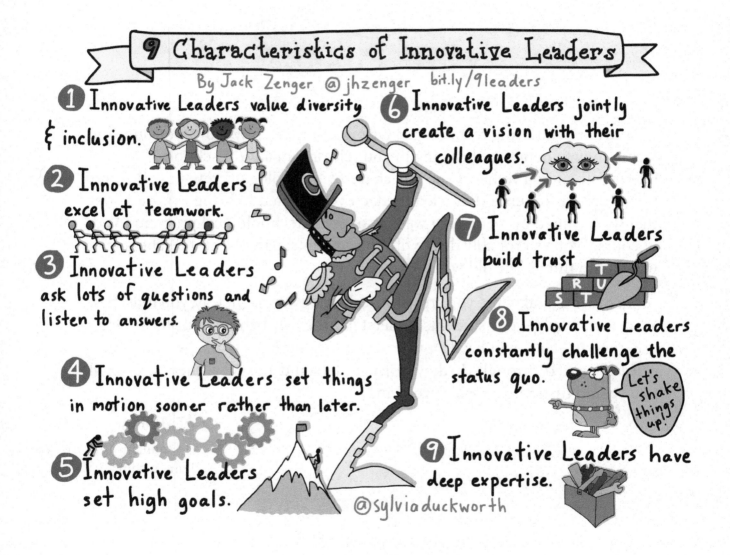

1 Innovative Leaders value diversity & inclusion.

2 Innovative Leaders excel at teamwork.

3 Innovative Leaders ask lots of questions and listen to answers.

4 Innovative Leaders set things in motion sooner rather than later.

5 Innovative Leaders set high goals.

6 Innovative Leaders jointly create a vision with their colleagues.

7 Innovative Leaders build trust

8 Innovative Leaders constantly challenge the status quo.

Let's shake things up!

9 Innovative Leaders have deep expertise.

@sylviaduckworth

7 WAYS TO USE TECHNOLOGY WITH PURPOSE

"Why are you using technology? Or more importantly, how are you using technology to better the learning in your classroom and/or school? If you are like me, then you've had your fair share of technology screw ups. Projects that didn't make sense (but used the tech you wanted to bring in). Activities that were ruined by a crashing website or some technological problem. And, of course, you've probably dealt with the students, parents, and teachers who want to do things 'the old way.'

"In order to make sure you are using technology the right way, you must first 'start with why.' If your students understand the *why* behind your technology use, then the class will have a purpose, and technological glitches and issues can be worked through. If they don't understand the *why*, then any small issue could turn into a major problem."

—AJ Juliani

@ajjuliani

ajjuliani.com

DOWNLOAD

bit.ly/sylsketch81

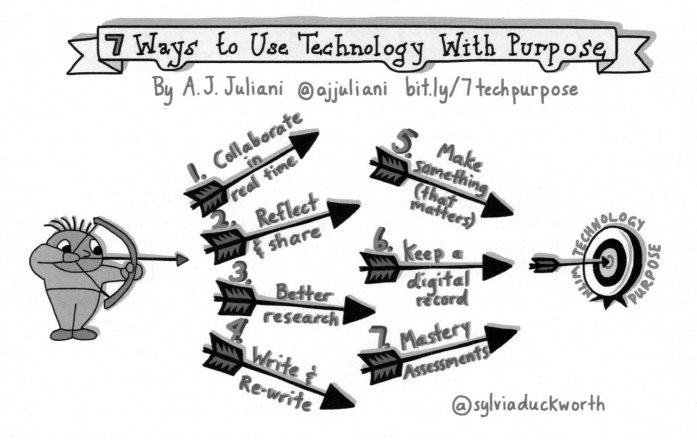

7 Ways to Use Technology With Purpose

By A.J. Juliani @ajjuliani bit.ly/7techpurpose

1. Collaborate in real time
2. Reflect & share
3. Better research
4. Write & Re-write
5. Make something (that matters)
6. Keep a digital record
7. Mastery Assessments

TECHNOLOGY PURPOSE

@sylviaduckworth

10 REASONS TO TEACH CODING

"Coding is a new literacy that holds tremendous importance for the future of our youth. By providing them with opportunities to think, take risks, be creative, and inquire about changing variables, we can better prepare them for success in a connected life."

—Brian Aspinall

@mraspinall

mraspinall.com

DOWNLOAD

bit.ly/sylsketch82

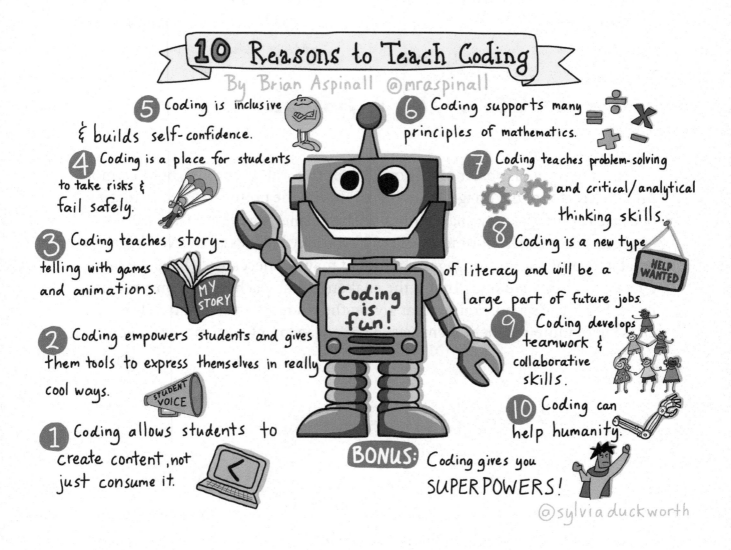

10 Reasons to Teach Coding

By Brian Aspinall @mraspinall

5 Coding is inclusive & builds self-confidence.

4 Coding is a place for students to take risks & fail safely.

3 Coding teaches story-telling with games and animations.

MY STORY

2 Coding empowers students and gives them tools to express themselves in really cool ways.

STUDENT VOICE

1 Coding allows students to create content, not just consume it.

Coding is fun!

6 Coding supports many principles of mathematics.

7 Coding teaches problem-solving and critical/analytical thinking skills.

8 Coding is a new type of literacy and will be a large part of future jobs.

HELP WANTED

9 Coding develops teamwork & collaborative skills.

10 Coding can help humanity.

BONUS: Coding gives you SUPERPOWERS!

@sylviaduckworth

LEVELS OF ENGAGEMENT

I saw the original poster of this on Twitter (by @alex_corbitt), but I cannot find the creator of the image. In any case, I found the premise to be fascinating because I could clearly visualize my students displaying these various levels of engagement at different times in class. It's a tricky business, however, because what may motivate and engage one student may not necessarily have the same effect on another student. That is the challenge that teachers face on a regular basis. For me, it's a no-brainer that giving the students a voice and a choice in class curriculum will help them rise to the engagement level more frequently.

—SD

DOWNLOAD
bit.ly/sylsketch90

Philip Schlecty's

Levels of Engagement

Drawn by @sylviaduckworth

ATTENTION + COMMITMENT = LEVEL OF ENGAGEMENT

HIGH ATTENTION	HIGH COMMITMENT	**ENGAGEMENT** · The student associates the task with a result or product that has meaning and value for the student. The student will persist in the face of difficulty and will learn at high and profound levels.
HIGH ATTENTION	LOW COMMITMENT	**STRATEGIC COMPLIANCE** - The task has little inherent or direct value to the student, but the student associates it with outcomes or results that do have value to the student (such as grades). Student will abandon work if extrinsic goals are not realized and will not retain what is learned.
LOW ATTENTION	LOW COMMITMENT	**RITUAL COMPLIANCE** - The student is willing to expend whatever effort is needed to avoid negative consequences. The emphasis is on meeting the minimum requirements. The student will learn at low and superficial levels.
NO ATTENTION	LOW COMMITMENT	**RETREATISM** · The student is disengaged from the task and does not attempt to comply with its demands, but does not try to disrupt the work or substitute other activities for it. The student does not participate and learns little or nothing from the task.
DIVERTED ATTENTION	NO COMMITMENT	**REBELLION** - The student refuses to do the work, acts in ways to disrupt others, or substitutes tasks & activities to which he or she is committed. Student develops poor work and sometimes negative attitudes towards formal education and intellectual tasks.

GARDNER'S MULTIPLE INTELLIGENCES THEORY

In 1983, Howard Gardner, an American psychologist, proposed the theory of multiple intelligences with which, by now, most teachers are quite familiar. There are many online tests to help determine these intelligences, but Gardner opposes the idea of labeling learners to one specific intelligence. Instead, he maintains that his theory of multiple intelligences should "empower learners" and encourage educators to approach teaching in different ways.

—SD

DOWNLOAD

bit.ly/sylsketch92

Gardner's Multiple Intelligences Theory

www.multipleintelligenceoasis.org

@sylviaduckworth

6 HURDLES FOR TEACHERS USING TECHNOLOGY

Why do some teachers embrace technology, yet others avoid it at all costs? This was a question I pondered when drawing this sketchnote. My idea was to provide some quick tips to help teachers get over some common hurdles to using technology.

—SD

DOWNLOAD
bit.ly/sylsketch99

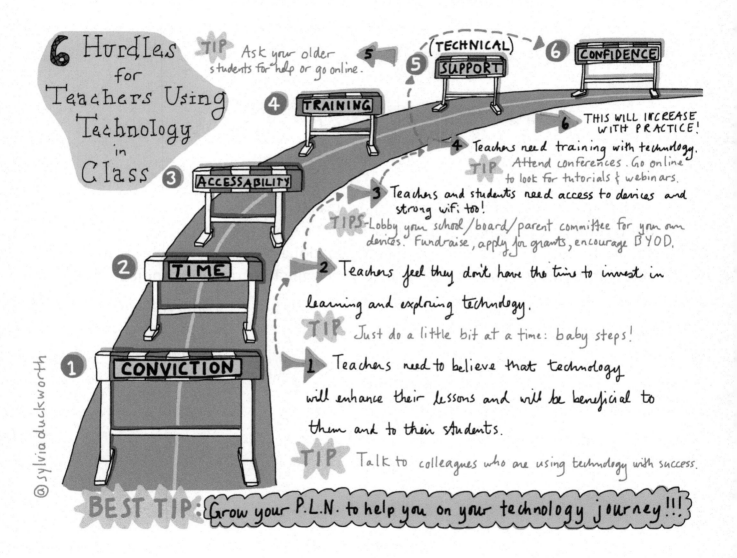

6 Hurdles for Teachers Using Technology in Class

1 CONVICTION
2 TIME
3 ACCESSABILITY
4 TRAINING
5 (TECHNICAL) SUPPORT
6 CONFIDENCE

TIP Ask your older students for help or go online.

6 THIS WILL INCREASE WITH PRACTICE!

4 Teachers need training with technology. TIP Attend conferences. Go online to look for tutorials & webinars.

3 Teachers and students need access to devices and strong wifi too! TIPS-Lobby your school/board/parent committee for your own devices. Fundraise, apply for grants, encourage BYOD.

2 Teachers feel they don't have the time to invest in learning and exploring technology. TIP Just do a little bit at a time: baby steps!

1 Teachers need to believe that technology will enhance their lessons and will be beneficial to them and to their students. TIP Talk to colleagues who are using technology with success.

@sylviaduckworth

BEST TIP: Grow your P.L.N. to help you on your technology journey!!!

THE PENCIL METAPHOR

"Regarding the pencil metaphor, most teachers (the wood) want to grow but feel they need help. This metaphor is not a matter of labeling people but should be seen as a tool for teachers to individually reflect on their current situation regarding any form of change, especially integrating technology."

—Richard Wells

@EDUWELLS
eduwells.com

DOWNLOAD
bit.ly/sylsketch93

Integrating Technology in Schools

THE PENCIL METAPHOR

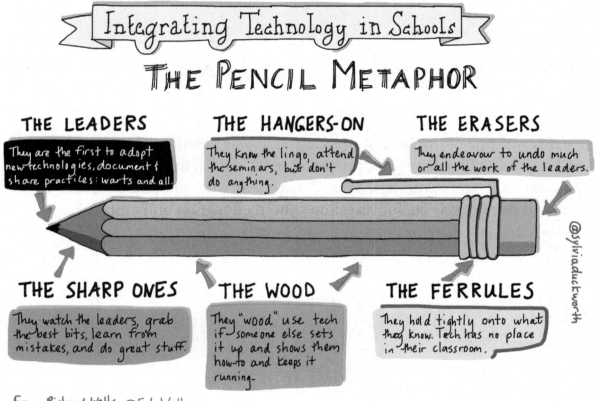

THE LEADERS
They are the first to adopt new technologies, document & share practices: warts and all.

THE HANGERS-ON
They know the lingo, attend the seminars, but don't do anything.

THE ERASERS
They endeavour to undo much or all the work of the leaders.

THE SHARP ONES
They watch the leaders, grab the best bits, learn from mistakes, and do great stuff.

THE WOOD
They "wood" use tech if someone else sets it up and shows them how-to and keeps it running.

THE FERRULES
They hold tightly onto what they know. Tech has no place in their classroom.

@sylviaduckworth

From Richard Wells @EduWells
Adapted from Lindy McKeown's idea.

SCHOOL VS LEARNING

This was one of my earliest drawings that was based on George's blog post at bit.ly/schoolvslearning. It provoked a lot of discussion on social media between educators who agreed and disagreed with the points made. These types of debates enrich conversations about education and emphasize why I believe that all educators should be on Twitter.

—SD

DOWNLOAD
bit.ly/sylsketch14

School vs Learning by George Couros

SCHOOL

- ☆ promotes starting by looking for answers
- ☆ is about consuming
- ☆ is about finding information on something prescribed for you
- ☆ teaches compliance
- ☆ is scheduled at certain times
- ☆ often isolates
- ☆ is standardized
- ☆ teaches us to obtain information from certain people
- ☆ is about giving you information
- ☆ is sequential A B C D E
- ☆ promotes surface-level thinking

@gcouros   bit.ly/schoolvslearning

LEARNING

- ☆ promotes starting with questions
- ☆ is about creating
- ☆ is about exploring your passions and interests
- ☆ is about challenging perceived norms
- ☆ can happen any time, all of the time
- ☆ is often social
- ☆ is personal
- ☆ promotes that everyone is a teacher and everyone is a learner
- ☆ is about making your own connections
- ☆ is random and non-linear
- ☆ is about deep exploration

@sylviaduckworth

For Our Students

PEOPLE KNOW
THEY MATTER WHEN

"Choose2Matter.org is a powerful call to action that challenges you...

* To ACCEPT that you matter, that you were created for significance, and that you have a contribution to make to the world.

* To ACT, by asking yourself, What matters most to me, and why? What breaks my heart about the world? and What am I going to do about it?

* To ACCELERATE the message that everyone matters.

So how, exactly, do you ACCELERATE this message? People know they matter when..."

—Angela Maiers

@angelamaiers
angelamaiers.com

DOWNLOAD

bit.ly/sylsketch06

People Know They Matter When...

By Angela Maiers

1. **You see them.**
   - ⭐ I hear you.
   - ⭐ I understand you.
   - ⭐ I appreciate you.
   - ⭐ It was great to spend time with you.
   - ⭐ I couldn't have done it without you.
   - ⭐ You made my day.
   - ⭐ You are a dear friend.

2. **You listen earnestly.**
   - ⭐ Open your 👀 and your ♥

3. **You ask meaningful questions**
   - ⭐ What's on your mind today?
   - ⭐ What was the best moment of your day?
   - ⭐ How did you make a difference today?
   - ⭐ What are your ambitions for this year?
   - ⭐ How can I help you achieve your goals?

4. **You believe they can.**
   - ⭐ When we encourage people to believe in themselves, we hand them the key to their own power.

5. **You dwell in possibility.**
   - ⭐ Envision the possibility to achieve the outcome. HOORAY!

6. **You celebrate them.**
   - ⭐ This reinforces their will to keep going.

7. **You do small things with GREAT love.**
   - you're great! High 5!

8. **You show up.**
   - I'm here!
   - ✓ Doing Good vs ✗ Doing Nothing

9. **You Choose2matter.**

bit.ly/angelapeoplematter   @sylviaduckworth

NO CHILD...

"When I was a teacher I had to get interested in student engagement quickly because my students, mostly from poverty, all living in a rural area in Texas, cared neither about my opinion of them nor about their grades. Pretty quickly, I figured out that if I wanted to garner their attention, a worksheet was not going to cut it. Later I taught advanced students, but I still had the same experience. If students felt the work mattered, they would get personally invested in it. This was still never true of a worksheet. That's when I realized no student has *ever* been personally invested in a worksheet and they never would be. I let worksheets go at that time. If there is no better way to teach something than a worksheet, it does not matter anyway."

—Amy Mayer

@friedtechnology
friedtechnology.com

DOWNLOAD

bit.ly/sylsketch07

10 REASONS TO USE TECHNOLOGY IN CLASS

It is wrong to use technology in class just for the sake of using technology. Here are some compelling reasons to use technology, mostly enabling students to do things which are difficult to do without technology.

—SD

DOWNLOAD
bit.ly/sylsketch10

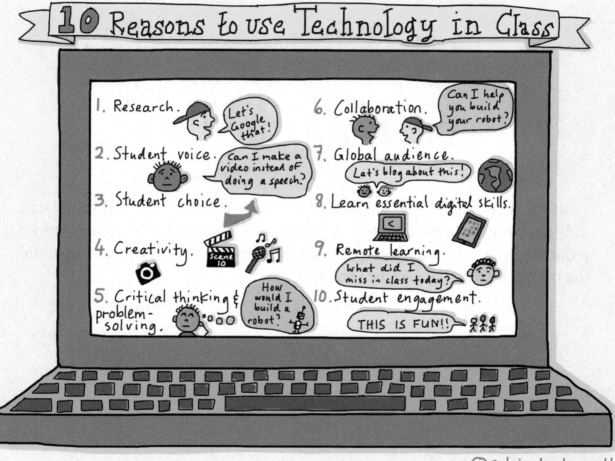

10 THINGS STUDENTS WANT EDUCATORS TO KNOW

"It's easy to forget what it's like to be a student, and at the end of the day, kids experience the same ups and downs of life as adults do. The more we (educators) can put ourselves in the shoes of our students, the more impactful the overall learning experience will be."

—Justin Tarte

@justintarte
justintarte.com

DOWNLOAD

bit.ly/sylsketch20

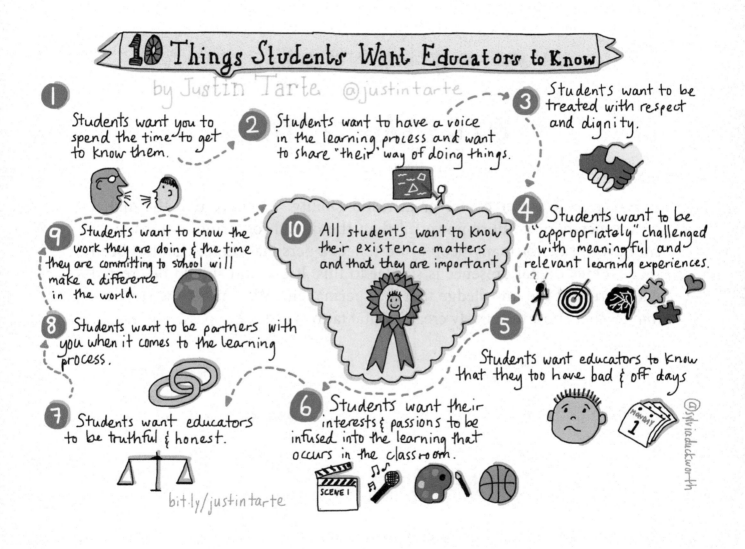

10 Things Students Want Educators to Know

by Justin Tarte @justintarte

1 Students want you to spend the time to get to know them.

2 Students want to have a voice in the learning process and want to share "their" way of doing things.

3 Students want to be treated with respect and dignity.

4 Students want to be "appropriately" challenged with meaningful and relevant learning experiences.

5 Students want educators to know that they too have bad & off days

6 Students want their interests & passions to be infused into the learning that occurs in the classroom.

7 Students want educators to be truthful & honest.

8 Students want to be partners with you when it comes to the learning process.

9 Students want to know the work they are doing & the time they are committing to school will make a difference in the world.

10 All students want to know their existence matters and that they are important

bit.ly/justintarte

@sylviaduckworth

117

DIGITAL TATTOO

"With great power comes great responsibility." I believe that the digital tattoo metaphor is more powerful than the digital footprint. Tattoos are a source of pride for many people and reflect a personal choice that has been made. One's digital presence is similar to this. It can and should be created with care and the knowledge that it is permanent. We must show students *and* teachers how to actively create digital tattoos instead of passively leaving digital footprints."

—Lee Araoz

@leearaoz
The Golden Age of Education

DOWNLOAD
bit.ly/sylsketch27

Your digital online presence is not a footprint...

@sylviaduckworth

It's a tattoo.  So make sure it's positive!

@LeeAraoz

TEACHING DIGITAL CITIZENSHIP

I have always been frustrated with teachers who refuse to embrace social media and who try to dissuade students from using it. Young people will always be on social media and they are using it at increasingly younger ages despite age restrictions. So why not teach them how to navigate it safely and responsibly? In addition, teachers themselves must be role models for the proper use of social media or they will have very little credibility or firsthand expertise.

—SD

DOWNLOAD

bit.ly/sylsketch29

We can't tell our students "Not to" use social media, or "Be careful" and then put our heads in the sand. Instead, we need to teach them how to be safe & responsible digital citizens (because they're going to be using it anyways.) @sylviaduckworth

10 WAYS CHILDREN ARE LIKE GARDENS

"It's important we meet children where they are. Each child is unique, and through nurturing they can grow and develop into confident adults. If nothing else, our mindfulness as educators can inspire these children, creating the most favorable environment for our students to flourish."

—Jessica Loucks

@JLenore24

DOWNLOAD

bit.ly/sylsketch38

10 Ways Children Are like Gardens

1. Children need nourishment: Love, encouragement, and hope.	1. Plants need nourishment: Sun, water, soil, and air.
2. Some children need more support than others.	2. Some plants need more support than others.
3. Every child is different and requires individual attention.	3. Every plant is different and requires individual attention.
4. A variety of children keeps life interesting.	4. A variety of plants keep a garden interesting.
5. Children need guidance and boundaries.	5. A garden needs pruning and weeding.
6. An ignored child will wilt and wane.	6. An ignored garden will wilt and wane.
7. Children need space to thrive.	7. A garden needs space to thrive.
8. Children will surprise you every day.	8. A garden will surprise you every day.
9. A happy child brings joy to everyone around him.	9. A plentiful garden can be enjoyed by many.
10. When we nurture a child, we reap the fruits of our labour when we see them flourish and soar.	10. When we nurture a garden, we reap the fruits of our labour when it flourishes and grows.

Inspired by the work of Dave Hotler, Jessica Loucks, and David Lee

@sylviaduckworth

123

6 GOLDEN RULES FOR ENGAGING STUDENTS

"Although many students are engaged at school, overall levels of engagement are quite low. This is an alarming situation because student engagement during school years not only contributes directly towards learning and achievement but also has a significant impact on adulthood (i.e., the people they become). This was the inspiration for my article as well as my career as engagement researcher."

—Nicolás Pino James

@npinojames
towardsengagement.com

DOWNLOAD

bit.ly/sylsketch49

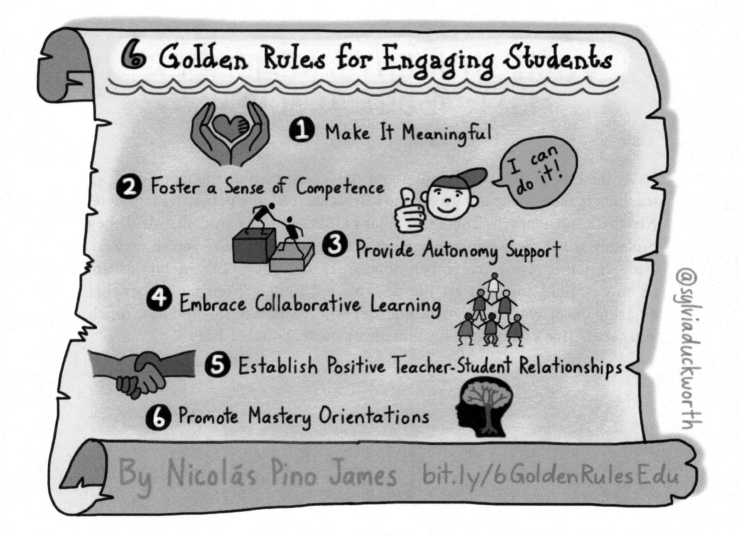

6 Golden Rules for Engaging Students

1. Make It Meaningful

2. Foster a Sense of Competence

I can do it!

3. Provide Autonomy Support

4. Embrace Collaborative Learning

5. Establish Positive Teacher-Student Relationships

6. Promote Mastery Orientations

By Nicolás Pino James   bit.ly/6GoldenRulesEdu

@sylviaduckworth

WHAT STUDENTS REMEMBER MOST ABOUT TEACHERS

"At the end of the day, it's not about the lesson plan or the fancy stuff we teachers make—the crafts we do, the stories we read, the papers we laminate. No, that's not really it. That's not what matters most to students. And they probably won't even remember what amazing lesson plans you've created. They certainly won't remember how organized your bulletin boards are or how straight and neat are the desk rows. No, they'll not remember that amazing decor you've designed. But they will remember you and how much you cared. That's what students remember most about teachers."

—Lori Gard

@lori_gard
pursuitofajoyfullife.com

DOWNLOAD
bit.ly/sylsketch54

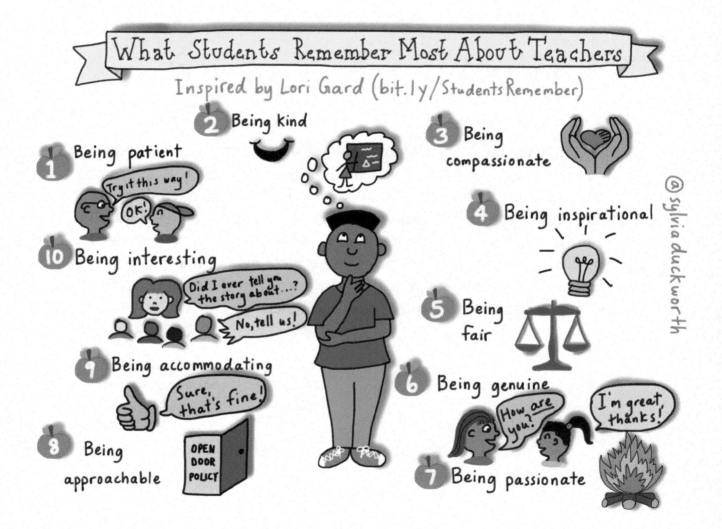

127

10 WAYS TO FLIP A KID

"First, I interviewed Kevin Honeycutt on my show, *Every Classroom Matters*. He mentioned flipping a kid, and I made a quote out of it. It went crazy everywhere I shared it. So, I was like, *OK, we can flip kids* and wrote a post. It was so popular. I can't remember who asked whom to do the sketchnote, but all I know is if Sylvia says she wants to draw something of mine, I always say yes. She has a way of pulling the heart of a topic. I believe that this post has done far better with her sketchnote than just words alone. It is a great example of how graphics and words make powerful partners."

—Vicki Davis

@coolcatteacher
coolcatteacher.com

DOWNLOAD
bit.ly/sylsketch55

129

CAREER ADVICE
FOR THE NEW ECONOMY

"We face a new economy, and so we have to ask new questions. Asking students what they want to be when they grow up is an old economy question. They can't possibly answer that question. There is a good chance their 'job' doesn't exist today. Asking them what problem do they want to solve is better suited for a network-based, knowledge-based, global economy."

—Jaime Casap

j@jcasap

jcasap.com

DOWNLOAD

bit.ly/sylsketch56

Career Advice for the New Economy

"Don't ask kids what they want to be when they grow up. Ask them what problems they want to solve and what they need to learn to be able to do that."

Jaime Casap @jcasap
Google Global Education Evangelist

@ sylviaduckworth

7 THINGS EVERY KID NEEDS TO HEAR

"Statistically speaking, I am supposed to be dead, in jail, or homeless.

"As a foster kid, my odds were already pretty bleak. About 20 percent of foster kids end up homeless. Less than 3 percent go on to earn a college degree. And only about half will be gainfully employed by the time they turn twenty-four years old.

"In addition to the fact that my odds were already not great, I was actively working to worsen my already bad situation. I was stubborn. I was making stupid choices. I was marvelously bitter. All at the ripe old age of fourteen.

"Yet here I am.

"Why? Because of my foster dad, Rodney.

"Because of ONE. CARING. ADULT.

"You see, *every kid is one caring adult away from being a success story.*"

—Josh Shipp
@joshshipp
joshshipp.com

DOWNLOAD

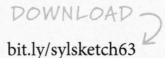

bit.ly/sylsketch63

"Every kid is ONE caring adult away from being a success story."
-Josh Shipp-

THE CONNECTED STUDENT

"My teaching practice has completely transformed as a result of being connected to other like-minded and passionate educators. As I became more and more passionate about student voice in the classroom and began to see how transformative these experiences for students could be, I tried to capture in writing all of the benefits that connected students experience. I love how Sylvia was able to visualize that blog post and those characteristics. Every student should have the opportunity to be connected."

—Jennifer Casa-Todd

@jcasatodd
jcasatodd.com

DOWNLOAD
bit.ly/sylsketch60

The Connected Student

By Jennifer Casa-Todd

CONNECTED STUDENTS...

Are more inclined to voice their opinions because they believe that their voices matter

Listen to me!

Are more engaged in school

Know that there are many people who can help them solve a problem & many different ways to do so

SOLUTION

Practice online collaboration and communication skills for audiences beyond their teacher

Understand how technology can connect them to experts and authors and have the confidence to reach out to them

Gain an understanding of other cultures & perspectives by building relationships and friendships with people from outside their communities

Utilize social media to create positive digital footprints

Recognize the power of social media to make a difference, change the status quo

WE CAN CHANGE THE WORLD!

bit.ly/jennconnected

@sylviaduckworth

135

EVERY CHILD NEEDS A CHAMPION

This is another epic, must-see video for all educators. The late, great, Rita Pierson embodied relational learning. She stressed, above all, the importance of making every child feel special. It's impossible to watch her TedTalk and not shed a tear. "Inspirational" is a huge understatement. It's simply awe-inspiring and will reaffirm your dedication to teaching with the heart.

—SD

DOWNLOAD

bit.ly/sylsketch65

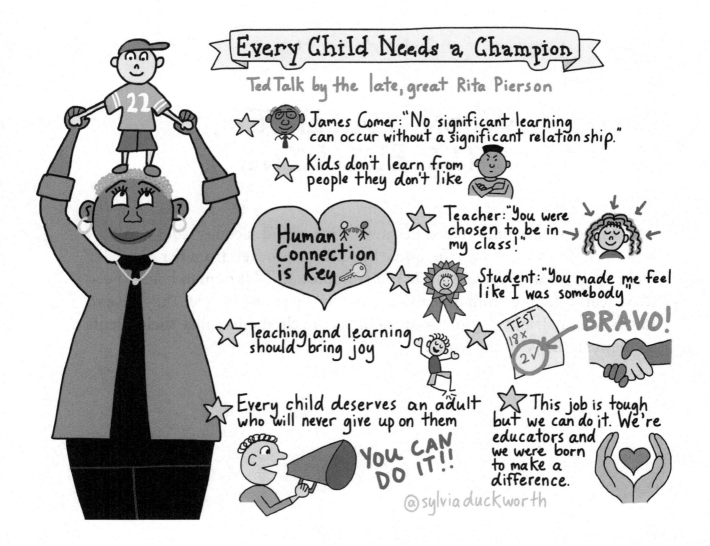

Every Child Needs a Champion

Ted Talk by the late, great Rita Pierson

James Comer: "No significant learning can occur without a significant relationship."

Kids don't learn from people they don't like

Human Connection is key

Teacher: "You were chosen to be in my class!"

Student: "You made me feel like I was somebody"

Teaching and learning should bring joy

TEST 18x 2✓ BRAVO!

Every child deserves an adult who will never give up on them

YOU CAN DO IT!!

This job is tough but we can do it. We're educators and we were born to make a difference.

@sylviaduckworth

WHEN YOU ENTER
THIS BUILDING

I first saw these lines in a slideshow of my friend Jacques Cool and they reminded me of the wonderful quote by Kathryn Stockett from her novel *The Help*: "You is kind. You is smart. You is important." All human beings need these reaffirmations from time to time, especially young people. They have so much potential, and our job as educators is to help them realize their talents so they can thrive in the world.

—SD

DOWNLOAD

bit.ly/sylsketch73

MOVING FROM DIGITAL CITIZENSHIP TO DIGITAL LEADERSHIP

"When I asked Sylvia if she had a sketchnote on the idea of digital leadership, she shared that she had one for digital citizenship. Together, we collaborated on the difference between digital citizenship and digital leadership (using George Couros' definition as a starting point). The bottom part of the sketchnote is the most important, and it came to us as we thought about how to guide teachers to get there. When we help kids to discover their passions and use social media and technology to share their learning, stand up for injustice, and become a more positive influence on others, we are moving beyond digital citizenship—we are helping kids to truly become leaders in the digital world."

—Jennifer Casa-Todd

@jcasatodd

jcasatodd.com

DOWNLOAD

bit.ly/sylsketch71

Moving from Digital Citizenship to Digital Leadership

Digital Citizenship: Using the Internet and Social Media in a responsible and ethical way

Digital Leadership: Using the Internet and Social Media to improve the lives, well-being and circumstances of others. - George Couros

I am a responsible Digital Citizen.
I use the internet and Social Media...

I am an inspirational Digital Leader.
I use the internet and Social Media...

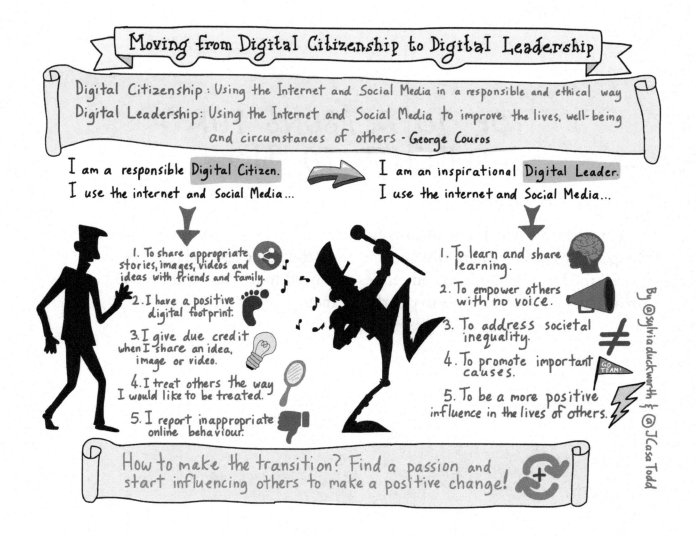

1. To share appropriate stories, images, videos and ideas with friends and family.

2. I have a positive digital footprint.

3. I give due credit when I share an idea, image or video.

4. I treat others the way I would like to be treated.

5. I report inappropriate online behaviour.

1. To learn and share learning.

2. To empower others with no voice.

3. To address societal inequality.

4. To promote important causes.

5. To be a more positive influence in the lives of others.

How to make the transition? Find a passion and start influencing others to make a positive change!

By @sylviaduckworth & @JCasaTodd

TOP 10 REASONS FOR STUDENTS TO BLOG

I created this sketchnote to convince teachers to *encourage* their students to blog and to convince administrators to *allow* their students to blog. The fear of social media is strong, and sometimes you need to lay out all the advantages in a visual manner like this to clearly see them.

—SD

DOWNLOAD
bit.ly/sylsketch79

Top 10 Reasons for Students to Blog

Blogging...

5 Gives students a voice

6 Teaches digital citizenship

4 Showcases student accomplishments

HOORAY!

7 Gives students a global and authentic audience

3 Improves writing and digital literacy

My Blog

8 Creates a digital portfolio

2 Establishes a home-school connection

9 Is cross-curricular

MATH
SOCIAL STUDIES
LANGUAGE ARTS
PHYS ED
SCIENCE
MUSIC
DRAMA
VISUAL ARTS

1 Promotes collaboration

10 Develops critical thinking skills

@sylviaduckworth

143

DON'T JUST TEACH KIDS
HOW TO COUNT

Similar to my drawing *Personal Qualities Not Measured by Tests*, this drawing emphasizes the need to teach and reinforce students' "soft skills," which will take them further in life than most academic curriculums.

—SD

DOWNLOAD
bit.ly/sylsketch83

Don't just teach kids how to count...

Teach them what counts.

5 Ps FOR A POSITIVE DIGITAL FOOTPRINT

The Queensland government in Australia produced a set of wonderful, child-friendly posters to promote a positive digital footprint. This drawing summarizes the important points and is perfect for introducing digital citizenship to children.

—SD

DOWNLOAD
bit.ly/sylsketch100

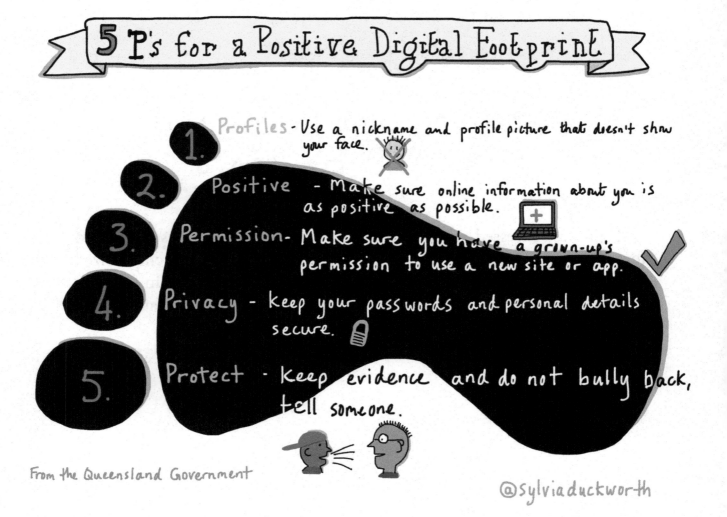

5 P's for a Positive Digital Footprint

1. **Profiles** - Use a nickname and profile picture that doesn't show your face.

2. **Positive** - Make sure online information about you is as positive as possible.

3. **Permission** - Make sure you have a grown-up's permission to use a new site or app.

4. **Privacy** - Keep your passwords and personal details secure.

5. **Protect** - Keep evidence and do not bully back, tell someone.

From the Queensland Government

@sylviaduckworth

147

PERSONAL QUALITIES NOT MEASURED BY TESTS

In the test-obsessed school culture of North America, it is so wrong to forget the more important qualities of children that should be emphasized and developed. Teachers, parents, and administrators need to join forces to stop the standardized testing movement that is destroying education in so many ways.

—SD

DOWNLOAD

bit.ly/sylsketch101

Personal qualities not measured by tests

Sense of wonder · Resourcefulness · Motivation · Creativity · Critical thinking · Self-discipline · Sense of beauty · Reliability · Empathy · Compassion · Self-awareness · Resilience · Endurance · Persistence · Determination · Grit · Spontaneity · Enthusiasm · Curiosity · Humor · Question asking · Humility · Courage · Civic Mindedness · Leadership · HA! HA! HA!

@sylviaduckworth

149

10 GROWTH MINDSET PHRASES

   I read about Carol Dweck's studies on growth mindset and was shocked to discover how damaging a teacher's praises can be if they focus on a student's perceived ability and not on his or her process for problem solving. I drew this to help teachers come up with alternative growth mindset phrases when praising students.

—SD

10 Growth Mindset Praises for Teachers to Give Students

The Golden Rule for Praise:

Praise Effort or Process NOT Ability or Trait

Instead of saying "You are so smart", try saying:

"I'm proud of you for giving it your best effort."

"I'm happy you figured that out for yourself!"

"You never gave up, even when it was hard."

"You have such a positive attitude!"

"What a creative solution to that problem!"

"Your hard work has really paid off!"

"You showed great perseverence reaching your goal."

"I admire you for trying so hard."

"I like the way you tried different strategies to figure that out."

"You are not afraid of a challenge: I like that!"

@sylviaduckworth

10 GROWTH MINDSET STATEMENTS

The original idea for this sketchnote was taken from a Tweet by @TerryHoganson. I'm not sure if he was the original author of these statements, but they're brilliant. I think that every teacher should review these statements with their students on a regular basis.

—SD

DOWNLOAD

bit.ly/sylsketch88

10 Growth Mindset Statements

FIXED MINDSET

GROWTH MINDSET

What can I say to myself?

INSTEAD OF:	TRY THINKING:
I'm not good at this.	1 What am I missing?
I'm awesome at this.	2 I'm on the right track.
I give up.	3 I'll use some of the strategies we've learned.
This is too hard.	4 This may take some time and effort.
I can't make this any better.	5 I can always improve so I'll keep trying.
I just can't do Math.	6 I'm going to train my brain in Math.
I made a mistake.	7 Mistakes help me to learn better.
She's so smart. I will never be that smart.	8 I'm going to figure out how she does it.
It's good enough.	9 Is it really my best work?
Plan "A" didn't work.	10 Good thing the alphabet has 25 more letters!

(Original source unknown)

@sylviaduckworth

For
Teachers

STAGNATION

I have little patience for teachers who refuse to step out of their comfort zone to try new things and who prefer, instead, to teach the same way year after year. That is what the teacher on the left of this drawing represents. The student on the right could also represent teachers who display a growth mindset. We need more teachers who are willing to learn and grow and adapt to today's constantly changing educational landscape.

—SD

DOWNLOAD

bit.ly/sylsketch01

"If you don't like change, you're going to like irrelevance even less."
-General Eric Shinseki

4 STAGES OF
TEACHER CONFIDENCE

"One of the biggest issues facing success with #edtech in education is that of teacher confidence. The 4 Stages of Teacher Confidence is one of the single most important ideas and resources I've come across to aid my thinking about how to work with educators to best support them in their learning journey to develop their use of technology in the classroom."

—Mark Anderson

@ICTevangelist
ictevangelist.com

DOWNLOAD
bit.ly/sylsketch12

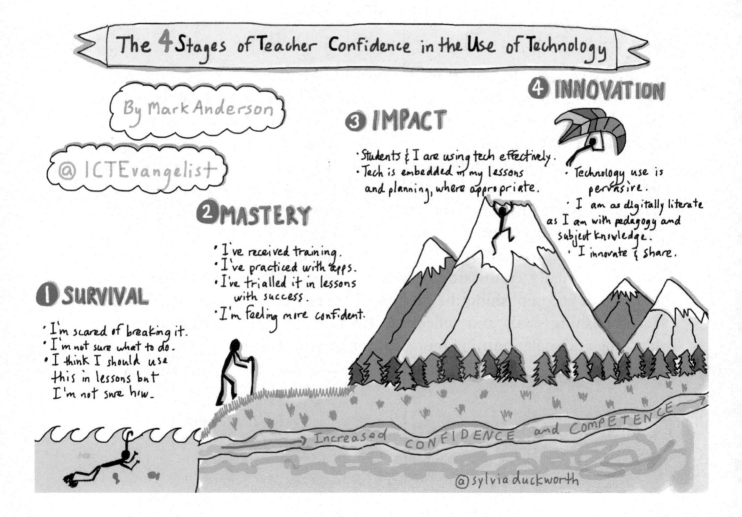

30 GOALS

"Every year, teachers worldwide accept the challenge to try to accomplish one to thirty instructional goals to improve the learning in their classrooms. This challenge is known as *The 30 Goals Challenge for Teachers* and has been in existence since January 2010. Each year, the goals will change, but the goals depicted in this sketchnote are the main goals written about in my book, *The 30 Goals Challenge for Teachers: Small Steps to Transform Your Teaching*. The goals cover various issues teachers face in the classroom, which include classroom management, connecting with students, partnering with parents, and integrating technology. Teachers accomplish a small, short-term goal, which is a small step towards an issue teachers tackle throughout the school year. After accomplishing the goal, teachers reflect on the impact. Through accomplishing goals and reflection, teachers are able to transform their teaching and make learning more meaningful for their learners."

—Shelly Terrell

@shellterrell

TeacherRebootCamp.com

DOWNLOAD

bit.ly/sylsketch70

Shelly Terrell's 30 Goals

1. Envision your greatness
2. Create your teaching Manifesto
3. Cultivate relationships
4. Partner with parents
5. Integrate Tech effectively
6. Show them how to navigate the web intelligently
7. Help them reflect on their online behavior
8. Reflect through a blog
9. Build a Teacher Survivor kit
10. Send them on a learner mission
11. Establish a web presence
12. Give students reign
13. Join an online educator community & develop a P.L.N.
14. Avoid burnout
15. Send a future message
16. Dare them
17. Re-evaluate value
18. Invite them in
19. Rethink student behavior & classroom management
20. Spread your message
21. Make it fun
22. Make a global connection
23. Plant a seed of belief
24. Change your environment
25. Collaborate with colleagues
26. Encourage play
27. Shake things up
28. Show your appreciation
29. Manifest an idea
30. Celebrate your achievements!

@sylviaduckworth

TEACHER'S PLEDGE

To me, this quote really encapsulates what our goal as teachers should be. It is unacceptable for a child to leave school with less interest in the world than when he or she began. Unfortunately, the problem is often systemic, and I believe that it is possible for a student to leave high school feeling discouraged despite having had some inspiring teachers. We need to change the school culture to one that encourages curiosity, risk-taking, and empowered students.

—SD

CONNECTION TO THE HEART

DOWNLOAD

bit.ly/sylsketch13

Teacher's Pledge

Our goal as educators should be...

...to ensure students leave more curiosity than when they arrived. that our school with

(paraphrased from Timberley, Kaser & Halbert)

If you have ever attended one of George's keynote speeches, you know that they are peppered with wonderful, insightful catch phrases that make ideal drawings. This was the first of many that I have drawn of George's quotes, and it is so true. If you cannot connect with a student on an emotional level, you will find it very hard to connect with him or her on any other level. This may take a herculean effort on your part for certain students, but it will pay off in huge dividends.

—SD

DOWNLOAD
bit.ly/sylsketch17

To inspire meaningful change, you must make a connection to the ♥ heart before you can make one to the mind — George Couros

@sylviaduckworth

HOW TO GROW A PLN

"I met Sylvia via my online network of great educators, and we have a profound mutual respect for each other's work. She brought forward the idea of sketchnoting my garden metaphor of a Professional or Personal Learning Network that expands 'organically.' We worked at it online with collaborative Google Docs and the result was quite astonishing. Reaching out to others in your PLN who share insights, promising practices, and valuable links is probably the most effective and sustainable form of PD."

—Jacques Cool

@zecool
zecool.com

DOWNLOAD
bit.ly/sylsketch21

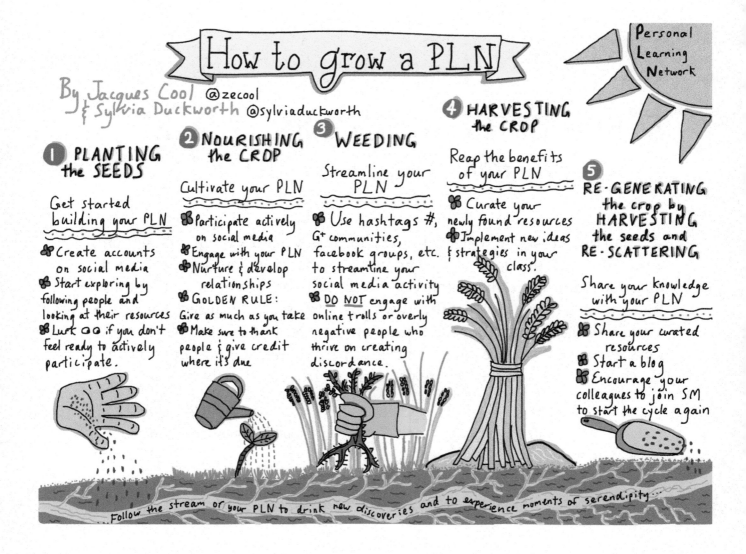

How to grow a PLN

By Jacques Cool @zecool
& Sylvia Duckworth @sylviaduckworth

Personal Learning Network

1 PLANTING the SEEDS

Get started building your PLN

❀ Create accounts on social media
❀ Start exploring by following people and looking at their resources
❀ Lurk 👀 if you don't feel ready to actively participate.

2 NOURISHING the CROP

Cultivate your PLN

❀ Participate actively on social media
❀ Engage with your PLN
❀ Nurture & develop relationships
❀ GOLDEN RULE: Give as much as you take
❀ Make sure to thank people & give credit where it's due

3 WEEDING

Streamline your PLN

❀ Use hashtags #, G+ communities, facebook groups, etc. to streamline your social media activity
❀ DO NOT engage with online trolls or overly negative people who thrive on creating discordance.

4 HARVESTING the CROP

Reap the benefits of your PLN

❀ Curate your newly found resources
❀ Implement new ideas & strategies in your class.

5 RE-GENERATING the crop by HARVESTING the seeds and RE-SCATTERING

Share your knowledge with your PLN

❀ Share your curated resources
❀ Start a blog
❀ Encourage your colleagues to join SM to start the cycle again

...Follow the stream of your PLN to drink new discoveries and to experience moments of serendipity...

5 POWERFUL QUESTIONS TEACHERS CAN ASK THEIR STUDENTS

"Many would agree that for inquiry to be alive and well in a classroom, amongst other things, the teacher needs to be expert at asking strategic questions, and not only asking well-designed ones, but ones that will also lead students to questions of their own. Over the years, I learned that asking straightforward, simply-worded questions can be just as effective as those intricate ones. If you are a new teacher or perhaps not so new but know that question-asking is an area where you'd like to grow, start with these five."

—Rebecca Alber

bit.ly/5questions4students
@wordlib

DOWNLOAD
bit.ly/sylsketch22

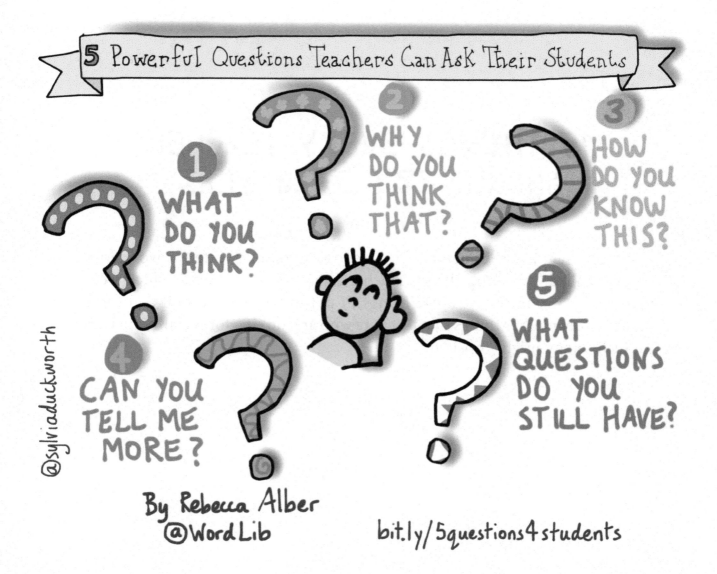

169

15 THINGS EVERY TEACHER SHOULD TRY THIS YEAR

Austin Gagnier, a Canadian high school student, tweeted a wonderful graphic called "15 Things Every Teacher Should Do This Year," which went viral on Twitter (bit.ly/Austin15Things). I put my own twist on it and came up with fifteen other things that teachers who are looking for meaningful uses for technology might consider.

—SD

DOWNLOAD

bit.ly/sylsketch23

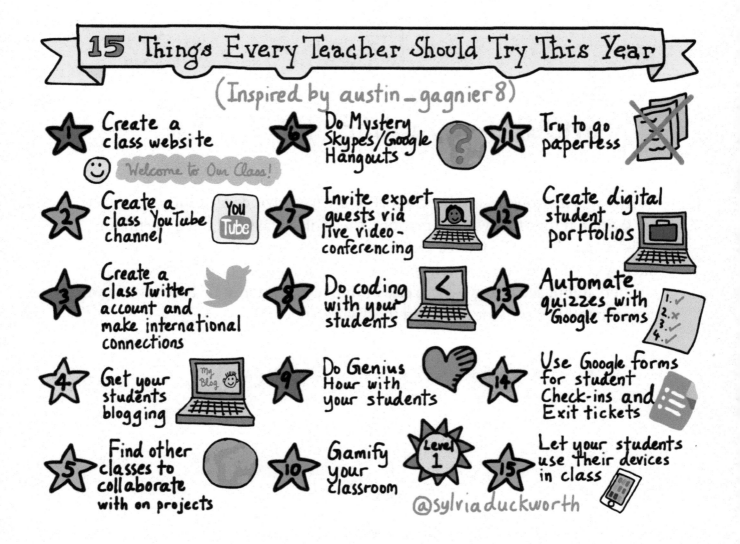

15 Things Every Teacher Should Try This Year

(Inspired by austin_gagnier8)

1. Create a class website — Welcome to Our Class!
2. Create a class YouTube channel
3. Create a class Twitter account and make international connections
4. Get your students blogging
5. Find other classes to collaborate with on projects
6. Do Mystery Skypes/Google Hangouts
7. Invite expert guests via live video-conferencing
8. Do coding with your students
9. Do Genius Hour with your students
10. Gamify your classroom
11. Try to go paperless
12. Create digital student portfolios
13. Automate quizzes with Google forms
14. Use Google forms for student Check-ins and Exit tickets
15. Let your students use their devices in class

@sylviaduckworth

SHOULD YOU USE TWITTER?

This was my tongue-in-cheek effort to try to convince all educators to get on Twitter. If they follow the directions, they will always end up in the middle, so why not sign up? I realize that teachers who first saw this drawing most likely were already on Twitter (since I tweeted it out), but it is possible that teachers might see it somewhere else online (e.g., Pinterest or Facebook) and consequently be convinced to join the Twittersphere.

—SD

DOWNLOAD
bit.ly/sylsketch24

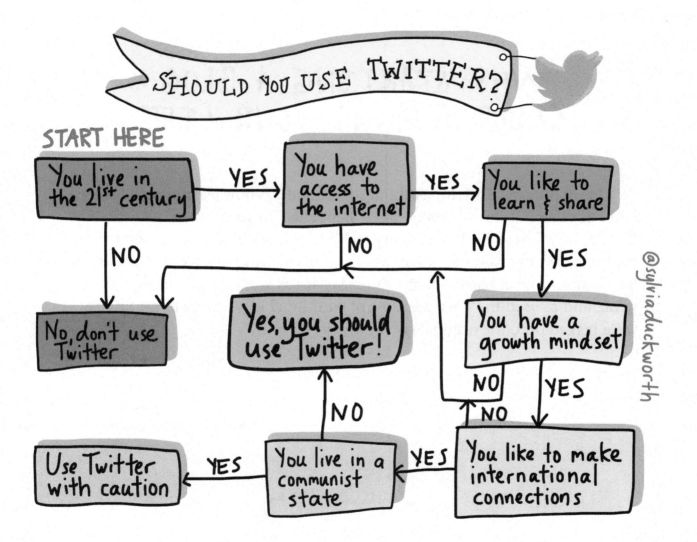

SHOULD YOU USE TWITTER?

START HERE

You live in the 21st century

YES → You have access to the internet

YES → You like to learn & share

NO → No, don't use Twitter

NO

NO

YES → You have a growth mindset

Yes, you should use Twitter!

NO → You live in a communist state

YES → Use Twitter with caution

YES → You like to make international connections

NO

NO

YES

@sylviaduckworth

WHY STARTING A BLOG
COULD CHANGE YOUR LIFE

"One of the powerful things about social media is how learning can escalate with the inspiration of others. Such happened to me. I read an article by Carolanne Johnson on Lifehack.org (bit.ly/carolanneblog). The content of her post inspired me to write one of my own, identifying the six elements from her post and what they meant to me. My focus was on education, and as I wrote and revised the post, a couple of additional ideas came to me and they were tagged onto the original six for my post."

–Doug Peterson

bit.ly/StartBlogDoug
@dougpete
dougpete.wordpress.com

DOWNLOAD
bit.ly/sylsketch28

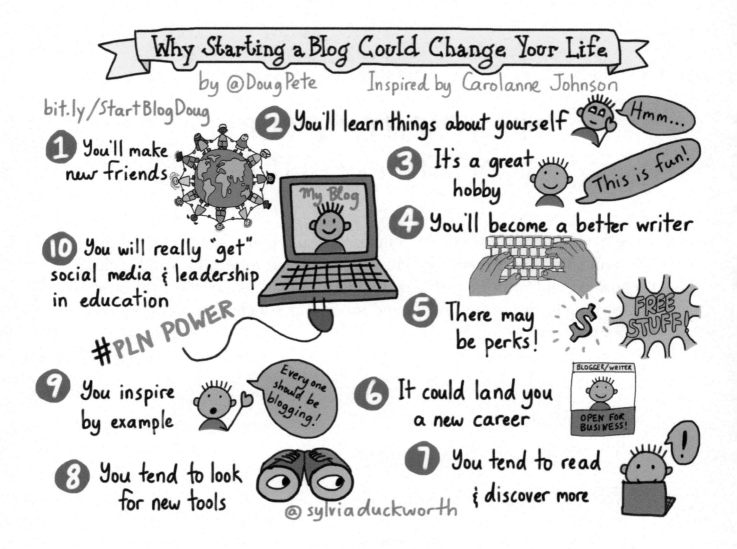

Why Starting a Blog Could Change Your Life

by @DougPete   Inspired by Carolanne Johnson

bit.ly/StartBlogDoug

1 You'll make new friends

2 You'll learn things about yourself   Hmm...

3 It's a great hobby   This is fun!

4 You'll become a better writer

10 You will really "get" social media & leadership in education

#PLN POWER

5 There may be perks!   FREE STUFF!

9 You inspire by example   Everyone should be blogging!

6 It could land you a new career   BLOGGER/WRITER   OPEN FOR BUSINESS!

8 You tend to look for new tools

7 You tend to read & discover more

My Blog

@sylviaduckworth

175

MY LEARNING CURVE
WITH TWITTER

Twitter has been a constant source of inspiration for me ever since I joined in 2011. I have made numerous international connections and lasting friendships, and I acquire new ideas for teaching daily. I drew this to illustrate my learning journey with Twitter and to try to persuade all educators to get on Twitter.

—SD

DOWNLOAD
bit.ly/sylsketch30

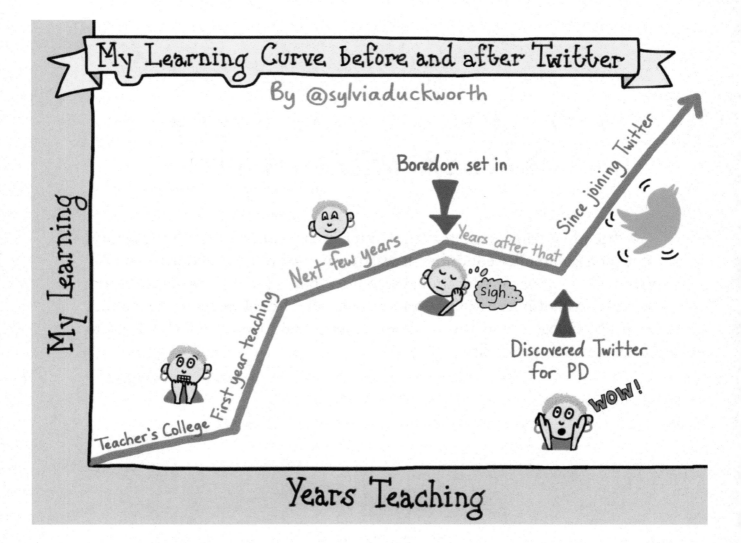

10 REASONS WHY EVERY TEACHER NEEDS A PLN

A friend convinced me to join Twitter in 2011, and I was very skeptical of what it could offer educators. It wasn't long before I realized that not only was it a holy grail for educational resources, but it was an easy and fast way to make instant international connections. Now I can't imagine life without my PLN. Google+ and Facebook are other social media platforms I use to connect with my PLN daily.

—SD

DOWNLOAD
bit.ly/sylsketch32

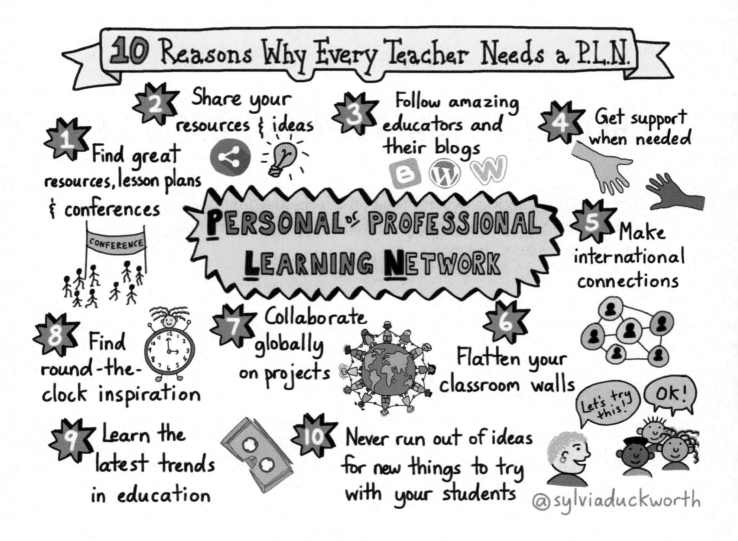

CHECKLIST FOR TODAY'S TEACHERS

I created this checklist when I took on a tech-coaching role at my school, and I started to think about what I wanted our teachers doing with our students. "Baby steps" is key!

—SD

DOWNLOAD
bit.ly/sylsketch39

A Checklist for Today's Teachers

☑ 1. My students have opportunities to be creative.

☑ 2. My students are allowed to display their learning in different ways.

☑ 3. My students document and reflect on their learning, exchange ideas and collaborate with others through blogging.

☑ 4. My students have digital portfolios to display their progress and to archive their work.

☑ 5. Guests are invited into our classroom (live or virtually) to broaden our knowledge and global perspective.

☑ 6. My students are aware of how to be safe online and how to be good digital citizens.

☑ 7. I model good digital citizenship by being present online and by connecting with others on social media.

☑ 8. I make an effort to connect face-to-face with other educators at conferences.

☑ 9. I model a growth mindset by stepping out of my comfort zone and trying new things.

☑ 10. I believe that I would enjoy being a student in my class.

@sylviaduckworth

12 WAYS TO RECHARGE
OVER THE HOLIDAYS

I don't really think that teachers need a list of things to do over the holidays. This was just my way of expressing why I love holidays so much and how I make the most of them. Of course, everyone's list will be different, but this is how I recharge my batteries to return to school refreshed and able to be a better teacher.

—SD

DOWNLOAD
bit.ly/sylsketch46

12 Ways to Recharge over the Holidays

@sylviaduckworth

1. Sleep in.
2. Get outside.
3. Read a good book.
4. Spend quality time with friends & family.
5. Exercise.
6. Get creative.
7. Indulge yourself.
8. Play.
9. Binge-watch a TV series.
10. Stay in pyjamas all day long.
11. Do nothing. Just do nothing
12. Reflect on your teaching and think of new things you will try next year.

10 WAYS TO MAINTAIN YOUR PASSION FOR TEACHING

I've been teaching for a very long time, and people who know me are in awe of how much I still love my job. So one day, I sat down to think about what the ingredients to a long and happy career in education might be. While I list a few factors in the drawing, I believe that the key to longevity is to have a growth mindset because if you are constantly trying new things, you will never be bored.

—SD

DOWNLOAD

bit.ly/sylsketch50

10 Ways to Maintain Your Passion For Teaching

2. Embrace change and try new things

3. Have fun in your class

4. Have a growth mindset

1. Be constantly curious

5. Embrace the uniqueness of each student

10. Be a connected educator

6. Learn from your students

7. Be flexible and open-minded

9. Attend conferences

8. Believe that you are making a difference in your students' lives

@sylviaduckworth

INSTRUCTIONAL COACHES

"Instructional coaches are the unsung heroes of the education profession. They nimbly navigate the line between administrator and teacher as they strive to make an impact across multiple grade levels and school sites. Instructional coaches have a unique vantage point—they see things happening at the ground level and are able to offer a perspective that few educators have."

—Lee Araoz

@leearaoz
thegoldenageofeducation.com

DOWNLOAD
bit.ly/sylsketch51

Instructional Coaches

By Lee Araoz @LeeAraoz

1. Provide job-imbedded professional development

2. Model and demonstrate best practices

3. Offer non-evaluative feedback on a regular basis

4. Are site-based teacher-leaders who support both teachers & students

GO TEAM!

5. Create an environment where student needs drive professional development

STUDENT NEEDS STUDENT NEEDS STUDENT

6. Offer guidance and feedback at the exact time teachers need it most

7. Inspire teachers to try new learning strategies and/or tools

8. Facilitate the transition from teacher-centered learning to learner-driven

TEACHER-CENTERED → LEARNER DRIVEN

@sylviaduckworth

WHAT MAKES A MASTER TEACHER?

"The term 'master teacher' seems to get thrown around a lot but is something that many educators aspire to be. In my ten years in the field of education, I would say that the definition of 'master teacher' has definitely changed. When I think of a master teacher, these are the qualities that I would suggest they have."

—George Couros

@georgecouros
georgecouros.ca

DOWNLOAD

bit.ly/sylsketch58

188

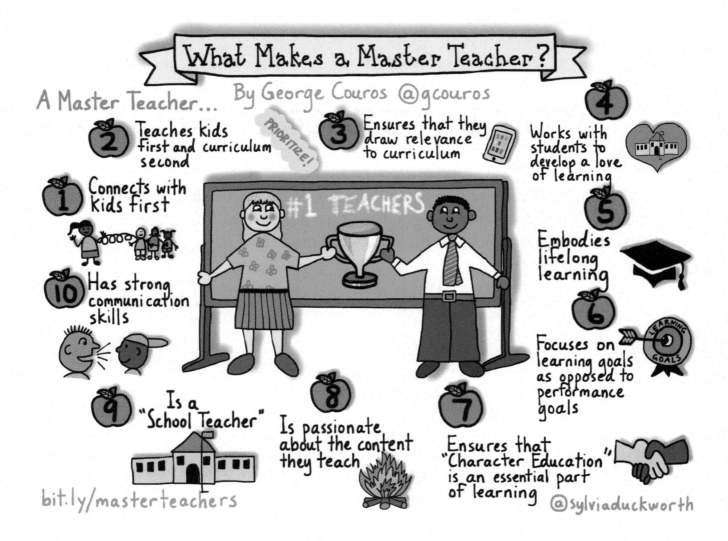

189

WHAT DO TEACHERS MAKE?

If you haven't yet seen Taylor Mali's video "What do Teachers Make?" on YouTube, stop what you're doing and go watch it (there are different versions). It's very moving, with a knockout message at the end.

—SD

DOWNLOAD

bit.ly/sylsketch62

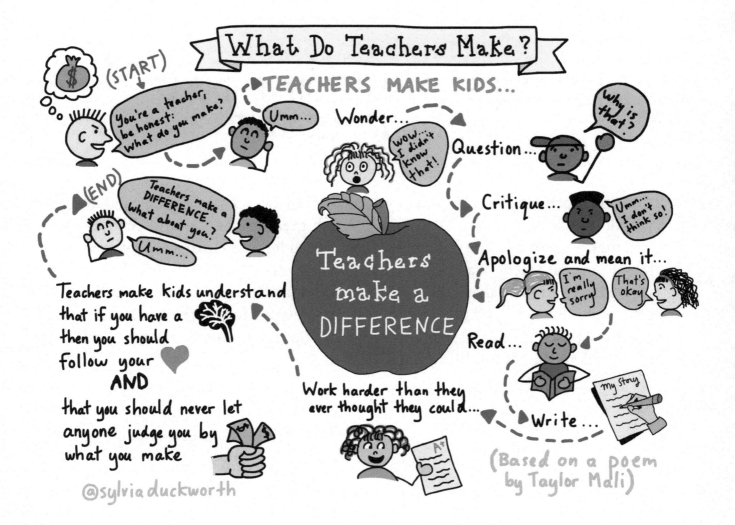

5 QUESTIONS YOU SHOULD ASK YOUR LEADER

"A great principal will help to develop great teachers, and a weak principal will do the opposite. They also tend to push great teachers out of schools, although most of the time unintentionally. Bad leaders tend to drive away great talent. A great teacher can become even better with a great principal. As the very wise Todd Whitaker says, 'when the principal sneezes, the whole school gets a cold.' Even though the questions were developed for superintendents to ask principals, I think that they should be questions any educator, parent, and even student should be able to openly ask their principal."

—George Couros

@georgecouros
georgecouros.ca

DOWNLOAD
bit.ly/sylsketch66

5 Questions You Should Ask Your Leader

By George Couros
@gcouros

@sylviaduckworth

1. Fostering Effective Relationships
What are some ways that you connect with your school community?

2. Instructional Leadership
What are some areas of teaching and learning that you can lead in the school?

3. Embodying Visionary Leadership
What are you hoping teaching and learning looks like in your school and how do you communicate that vision?

4. Developing Leadership Capacity
How do you build leadership in your school?

5. Creating Sustainable Change
What will be your "fingerprints" on this building after you leave?

bit.ly/5leaderquestions

12 THINGS I LOVE ABOUT THE SUMMER HOLIDAYS

I never got into teaching because of the summer holidays, but boy, do I ever appreciate them! As rewarding as teaching is, it is also intense, demanding, and exhausting. Holidays allow us to recharge and reflect on our profession so that we can return the following year, energized to inspire our students and to give them our very best.

—SD

DOWNLOAD
bit.ly/sylsketch74

12 Things I love about the Summer Holidays

By @sylviaduckworth, teacher

1 Stress-Free Sunday nights

2 Being able to stay up late

3 No mad morning rush

4 Staying in my pyjamas as long as I want

5 Not knowing what day it is

6 No marking!

7 Having time to reflect on my practice, explore new ideas, and attend PD sessions

8 Eating slowly YUM!

9 Going to the bathroom whenever I want

10 Finishing a cup of coffee before it gets cold (or spills)

11 Getting lost in a good book

12 More time to spend with friends and family and to do some things I love to do.

AS A TEACHER

"The teacher has the power to change, shape, and mold young people's lives on a daily basis. Never underestimate your impact and influence on their lives. Teachers are more valuable than they realize and have an everlasting impression."

—Mark Martin

@Urban_teacher
urbanteacher.co.uk

DOWNLOAD

bit.ly/sylsketch75

As a teacher, you have the ability to change...

A story
A mind
A direction
A path
An environment
A future
A situation
A life.

By @Urban_Teacher   Drawn by @sylviaduckworth

10 THINGS TEACHERS WANT FOR PROFESSIONAL DEVELOPMENT

Someone on Twitter once asked me, "Where is the research that supports the statements in this drawing?" My answer: thirty-plus years of teaching and sitting in some excruciatingly irrelevant mandatory personal development (P.D.) sessions. If you have ever said to yourself, *What a waste of time. This does not apply to me or my students, and I have a million other things I could be doing right now*, you can probably relate. I hope that administrators will use this drawing to rethink how P.D. is delivered in their schools.

—SD

DOWNLOAD
bit.ly/sylsketch80

10 Things Teachers Want for Professional Development

5 Teachers want P.D. that is innovative and creative.

4 Teachers want P.D. that is conducted by professionals with classroom experience.

3 Teachers want P.D. that they can use right away.

2 Teachers want P.D. that is relevant for their students.

1 Teachers want a voice and a choice in the P.D. offered.

6 Teachers want P.D. that makes them better teachers.

7 Teachers want P.D. that is practical, not theoretical.

8 Teachers want P.D. that allows them to collaborate and speak honestly.

9 Teachers want P.D. that will be relevant for a long time.

10 Teachers want admin to attend and to participate in the P.D. sessions.

@sylviaduckworth

I TEACH

    This drawing was inspired by a poster by Krissy Venosdale, and I think it well reflects the idea that teachers do so much more than just impart information. I added "I am connected" because "I learn every day" is facilitated when you have a PLN.

—SD

DOWNLOAD

bit.ly/sylsketch85

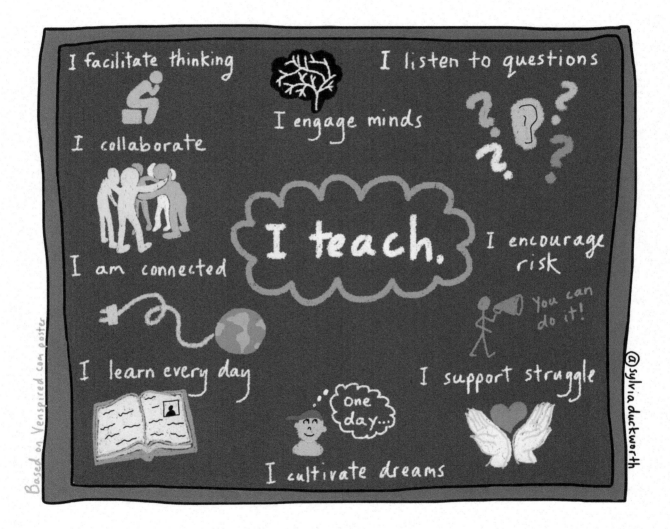

10 THINGS TEACHERS WANT PARENTS TO KNOW

I was inspired to draw this after I read a blog post titled, "Dear Teachers: Here are 10 Things Every Parent Wants You to Know." I'm sure I missed a few, but these are what are important to me.

—SD

DOWNLOAD

bit.ly/sylsketch96

10 Things Teachers Want Parents to Know

Dear parents,   Any school

   Please,

1. If your child is young, please read to him/her every night.

2. Allow me to hold your child accountable for his/her actions.

3. Your child's homework is not your responsibility. It is his/hers.

4. Keep in mind that I am a professional and that I have the
   best interests of your child in mind.

5. We are on the same team. I also want your child to flourish and be happy.

6. Be aware that your attitude towards me will influence your child's attitude.

7. It is okay for your child to experience failure. It is how he/she will grow.

8. Give your child time to play with no agenda. Playing outside is even better.

9. Talk to me before talking to the administration if you have any concerns.

10. Encourage your child to be his/her own advocate. →
        Sincerely, your child's teacher.

HOMEWORK
Math p.2-4
Novel - read
chapter 3

@ Sylvia Duckworth

8 CHARACTERISTICS OF THE INNOVATOR'S MINDSET

"The innovator's mindset is the belief that abilities, intelligence, and talents are developed, leading to the creation of new and better ideas.

"To develop students as 'innovators' in their pursuits, we must embody this as educators first, and then embody this Mindset as a school culture. Looking at different processes where innovation excels, such as design thinking, there are several characteristics that seem common amongst these themes."

—George Couros

@georgecouros
georgecouros.ca

DOWNLOAD

bit.ly/sylsketch97

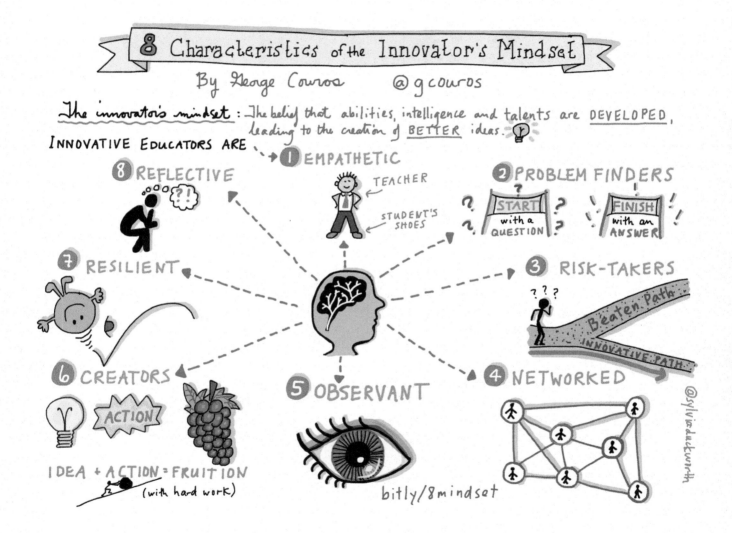

8 Characteristics of the Innovator's Mindset

By George Couros   @gcouros

The innovator's mindset: The belief that abilities, intelligence and talents are DEVELOPED, leading to the creation of BETTER ideas.

INNOVATIVE EDUCATORS ARE

1 EMPATHETIC
TEACHER
STUDENT'S SHOES

2 PROBLEM FINDERS
START with a QUESTION
FINISH with an ANSWER

3 RISK-TAKERS
Beaten Path
INNOVATIVE PATH

4 NETWORKED

5 OBSERVANT
bitly/8mindset

6 CREATORS
ACTION
IDEA + ACTION = FRUITION
(with hard work)

7 RESILIENT

8 REFLECTIVE

@sylviaduckworth

205

Google!

THINGS GOOGLE TEACHERS
NEVER HEAR

"Until I started using Google Apps in my classroom, so much of my time was spent dealing with logistics required for learning, rather than actual learning. Lost work, missing work, inability to complete assignments because of a lack of resources. Now that I work in a school that is BYOD with Google Apps, so many of the logistical issues I used to deal with have evaporated. Now we can spend more time doing what got me into teaching in the first place."

—Kevin Brookhouser
@brookhouser
kevinbrookhouser.com

DOWNLOAD
bit.ly/sylsketch09

Things Google Teachers Never Hear

Inspired by Kevin Brookhouser & Amy Burvall

6 "My assignment is on a USB key that I lost."

5 "Oh darn, this isn't the updated version of my assignment!"

7 "Do you have a stapler?"

4 "I can't work on the assignment at home because I don't have the software."

8 "My partner has the assignment and he's not here."

3 "My printer is broken/ran out of ink/ran out of paper."

9 "We're doing a group project but we can't figure out a time to get together."

2 "I finished my assignment but it's on my computer at home."

10 "I emailed the assignment to myself but I never got it."

1 "I forgot to save my work."

11 "My dog ate my assignment."

bit.ly/kevinneverhear   bit.ly/amyburvall

@sylviaduckworth

THE GAFE TRAIN

I was inspired to do this drawing when I realized that more and more educators and students are using Google Apps for Education (GAFE). And why not? They are the best platform for collaboration, and they are *free*! Teachers who are not on the GAFE train yet will hopefully soon get on board because there are many stations they will not want to miss!

—SD

DOWNLOAD

bit.ly/sylsketch15

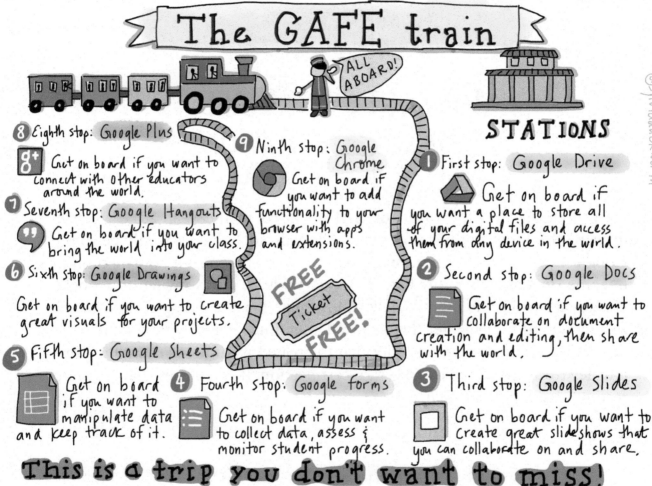

The GAFE train

@sylviaduckworth

"ALL ABOARD!"

STATIONS

8 Eighth stop: Google Plus
Get on board if you want to connect with other educators around the world.

7 Seventh stop: Google Hangouts
Get on board if you want to bring the world into your class.

6 Sixth stop: Google Drawings
Get on board if you want to create great visuals for your projects.

5 Fifth stop: Google Sheets
Get on board if you want to manipulate data and keep track of it.

9 Ninth stop: Google Chrome
Get on board if you want to add functionality to your browser with apps and extensions.

FREE Ticket FREE!

4 Fourth stop: Google Forms
Get on board if you want to collect data, assess & monitor student progress.

1 First stop: Google Drive
Get on board if you want a place to store all of your digital files and access them from any device in the world.

2 Second stop: Google Docs
Get on board if you want to collaborate on document creation and editing, then share with the world.

3 Third stop: Google Slides
Get on board if you want to create great slideshows that you can collaborate on and share.

This is a trip you don't want to miss!

7 STAGES OF GAFE IMPLEMENTATION

My journey into the world of GAFE started in the year 2011 when a forward-thinking administrator at my school decided that we would be going Google. It was a tough transition for many staff members, but now we cannot imagine (or remember) life before GAFE. In 2012, I was invited to Google Headquarters in Mountain View, California, for the Google Innovator's Academy, and shortly after that I started attending GAFE Summits, first as a delegate, then as a presenter. I decided to create this drawing describing my journey from GAFE novice to GAFE certification. It's a journey that I cannot recommend highly enough.

—SD

DOWNLOAD

bit.ly/sylsketch16

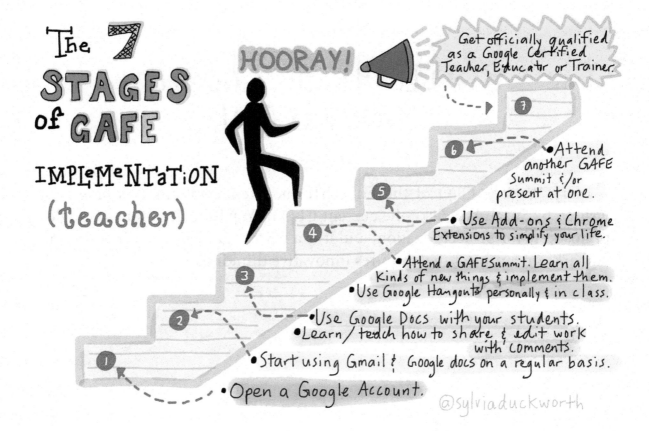

The 7 STAGES of GAFE IMPLEMENTATION (teacher)

HOORAY!

Get officially qualified as a Google Certified Teacher, Educator or Trainer.

7
6 • Attend another GAFE Summit &/or present at one.
5 • Use Add-ons & Chrome Extensions to simplify your life.
4 • Attend a GAFE Summit. Learn all kinds of new things & implement them. • Use Google Hangouts personally & in class.
3 • Use Google Docs with your students. • Learn/teach how to share & edit work with comments.
2 • Start using Gmail & Google docs on a regular basis.
1 • Open a Google Account.

@sylviaduckworth

8 PILLARS OF GOOGLE INNOVATION

Mark Wagner, CEO of the EdTechTeam, often mentions this blog post written by Susan Wojcicki, the current CEO of YouTube. It outlines Google's philosophy for project ideation, and it is a perfect guideline for anyone who embarks on a project that requires innovative thinking.

—SD

DOWNLOAD
bit.ly/sylsketch31

The 8 Pillars of Google Innovation

By @SusanWojcicki   bit.ly/8GooglePillars

@sylviaduckworth

1 Have a mission that matters.
2 Think big but start small.
3 Strive for continual innovation, not instant perfection.
4 Look for ideas everywhere.
5 Share everything.
6 Believe the impossible.
7 Be a platform.
8 Never fail to fail.

25 OF MY FAVOURITE GOOGLY THINGS

I am a huge fan of all things Google, and these are some of my favourite things in alphabetical order. For a complete list, please visit bit.ly/SylFaveGoogly.

—SD

DOWNLOAD
bit.ly/sylsketch33

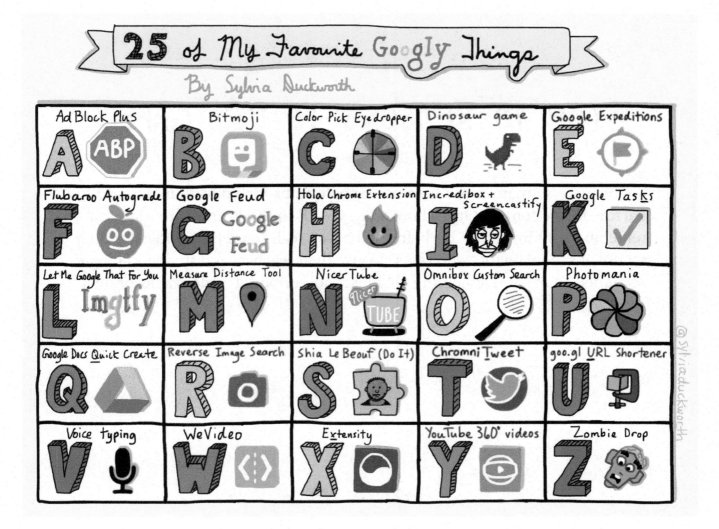

TOP 10 REASONS TO USE GAFE

There are so many reasons to use Google Apps for Education, it's hard to narrow to the top 10. Our school went GAFE in 2011, and I honestly can't remember—or imagine—life before it. I have a really hard time understanding school or school boards who refuse to give their teachers and students Google accounts. To me, implementing GAFE school- or board-wide is a no-brainer.

—SD

DOWNLOAD

bit.ly/sylsketch76

Top **10** Reasons to Use G.A.F.E.

1. Unlimited storage.

2. Documents are saved automatically. HOORAY!!

3. Live-time collaborating & sharing on documents.

4. Chrome Apps & Extensions tools to create with.

5. Access your Drive and Chrome bookmarks from anywhere in the world, on any device.

Google Apps for Education

6. Google Drive Add-ons to automate your workload. Thanks, Google, for giving me more time to do the things I love!

7. Easy data collection with Google Forms. Ugh... can't open this document!

8. Immediate feedback on documents with chat, comments, & suggested edits.

9. No software required.

10. It's free. FREE

@sylviaduckworth

THE 9 ELEMENTS OF DIGITAL CITIZENSHIP

This drawing is based on a blog post written by Mike Ribble. It is so important to teach students all aspects of digital citizenship to keep them safe in the dangerous World Wide Web. Teachers, parents, and administrators should also be reminded of these safeguards from time to time.

—SD

DOWNLOAD

bit.ly/sylsketch86

The 9 Elements of Digital Citizenship

on the WEB

5 DIGITAL ETIQUETTE
Do students know when to use technology appropriately & always in a positive manner?

4 DIGITAL LITERACY
Do students know how to use various digital techologies and how to assess legitimacy of web resources?

6 DIGITAL LAW
Do students understand how to use and share digital content legally & how to respect content ownership by citing sources?

3 DIGITAL COMMUNICATION
Do students understand what is appropriate to share through email, texting, video chatting & social media?

7 DIGITAL RIGHTS & RESPONSIBILITIES
Do students understand that they have a right to safe & friendly digital communications and a responsibility to report instances that threaten this?

2 DIGITAL COMMERCE
Are students aware of the dangers and benefits of buying and selling online?

"With great power comes great responsibility"
-SPIDERMAN

8 DIGITAL HEALTH
Are students aware of the physical and psychological dangers of excessive internet usage?

1 DIGITAL ACCESS
Are educators & students aware that not everyone has equal access to technology resources?
(Based on the work of Mike Ribble)

9 DIGITAL SECURITY
Do students know how to stay safe by using difficult passwords, virus protection, backing up data, and being aware of identity theft, phishing, & other online scams?

@Sylviaduckworth
@courosa

GOOGLE DOCS SHARING PERMISSIONS

I love Google docs, but the sharing options can get a little complicated, so I drew up this graph to simplify it. No more guessing!

—SD

DOWNLOAD

bit.ly/sylsketch87

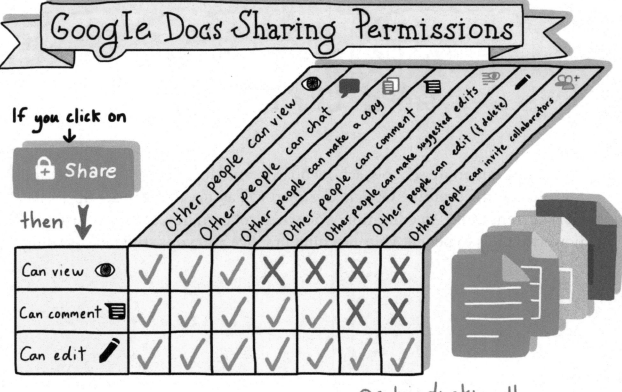

Google Docs Sharing Permissions

If you click on ↓

🔒 Share

then ↓

	Other people can view	Other people can chat	Other people can make a copy	Other people can comment	Other people can make suggested edits	Other people can edit (& delete)	Other people can invite collaborators
Can view 👁	✓	✓	✓	✗	✗	✗	✗
Can comment	✓	✓	✓	✓	✓	✗	✗
Can edit ✏	✓	✓	✓	✓	✓	✓	✓

@sylviaduckworth

10 REASONS TO GET
GAFE CERTIFIED

As more and more schools, school boards, and districts adopt Google Apps for Education, becoming Google Certified will assure that you are up-to-date with current trends in education. You will also learn how best to utilize these powerful tools to benefit your teaching practice and your students' learning.

DOWNLOAD
bit.ly/sylsketch102

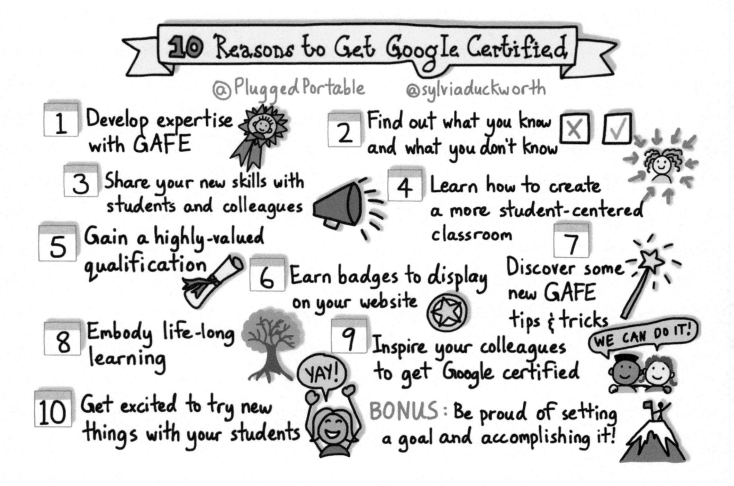

BOOK SYLVIA DUCKWORTH TO SPEAK AT YOUR NEXT TEACHER PROFESSIONAL DEVELOPMENT SESSION OR CONFERENCE!

Sylvia's popular sessions include...

The Talent Myth

Are we born with natural talent or can we develop skills with determination and hard work? What are the implications of the nurture vs nature argument in education? How do we encourage a growth mindset amongst ourselves *and* our students? Using Matthew Syed's book *Bounce* as a guideline, Sylvia explores these questions while she describes her journey from non-artist to sketchnoting fanatic.

Why Creativity Matters

What are the benefits of creativity in education and on a personal level? How do we encourage creativity amongst our students and foster our own creative endeavours? Using some of her sketchnotes as illustrations, Sylvia answers these questions as she reflects on the importance of creativity in our professional and personal lives. At the end of her session she will share some secrets for sketchnoting, so come prepared to do some drawing!

How to Survive (and Thrive) in the Digital Age of Education

The educational landscape has changed dramatically in the last few years due to technology. How do we remain relevant to our students in this new world? How do we manage the paradigm shift from teachers as content providers to learning facilitators? What are some tips for keeping up with technology? These are a few essential questions that Sylvia explores during this talk.

Empowering the Introvert

Up to half of the population are introverts. Are we doing enough in our classrooms to accommodate the introverted student? What are some tips for introverts to minimize social and performance anxiety? How can you alter your body language to better manage a stressful situation? How can technology and social media help introverts express themselves in non-threatening ways? As educators, should we reconsider "class participation" grades? A self-confessed introvert herself, Sylvia speaks from the heart during this frank talk.

How to Maintain Your Passion for Teaching

Have you reached a plateau in your teaching? Are you missing the "zip" in your lesson plans? Are you in need of some concrete ideas to re-energize your class and fall in love with teaching again? Join Sylvia as she lets you in on her tips and tricks for maintaining a passion for teaching and keeping your students engaged. With more than thirty years of teaching experience under her belt, Sylvia can speak with authority on this subject.

The Connected Educator

What is a *connected educator*? How do you grow your *personal learning network*? What are some of the benefits of making global connections personally and professionally? Sylvia will walk session participants through the social media tools necessary to become a connected educator and will help you get started on different platforms. We will also learn about the importance of teaching digital citizenship to your students to move them from responsible and safe digital citizens to empowered global digital leaders.

For more information visit EdTechTeam.com/books

To request a workshop or for more info
contact press@edtechteam.com

MORE BOOKS FROM EdTechTeam PRESS

EDTECHTEAM.COM/BOOKS

THE HYPERDOC HANDBOOK
Digital Lesson Design Using Google Apps
By Lisa Highfill, Kelly Hilton, and Sarah Landis

The HyperDoc Handbook is a practical reference guide for all K–12 educators who want to transform their teaching into blended-learning environments. This bestselling book strikes the perfect balance between pedagogy and how-to tips, while also providing ready-to-use lesson plans to get you started with HyperDocs right away.

THE GOOGLE APPS GUIDEBOOK
Lessons, Activities, and Projects Created by Students for Teachers
By Kern Kelley and the Tech Sherpas

The Google Apps Guidebook is filled with great ideas for the classroom from the voice of the students themselves. Each chapter introduces an engaging project that teaches students (and teachers) how to use one of Google's powerful tools. Projects are differentiated for a variety of age ranges and can be adapted for most content areas.

ASSESSMENT THAT MATTERS
Using Technology to Personalize Learning
By Kim Meldrum

In *Assessment That Matters,* Kim Meldrum explains the three types of assessment—assessment *as* learning, assessment *for* learning, and assessment *of* learning. Within her instruction on gathering rich assessment information, you'll find simple strategies and tips for using today's technology to allow students to demonstrate learning in creative and innovative ways.

THE SPACE
A Guide for Educators

By Rebecca Louise Hare and Robert Dillon

The Space takes the current conversation about reshaping school spaces to the next level. This book goes well beyond the ideas for learning-space design that focus on Pinterest-perfect classrooms and instead discusses real and practical ways to design learning spaces that support and drive learning.

A LEARNER'S PARADISE
How New Zealand Is Reimagining Education

By Richard Wells

What if teachers were truly trusted to run education? In *A Learner's Paradise*, Richard Wells describes New Zealand's forward-thinking education system in which teachers are empowered to do exactly that. With no prescribed curriculum, teachers and students work together to create individualized learning plans—all the way through the high school level. From this guidebook, you'll learn how New Zealand is reimagining education and setting an example for innovative educators, parents, and school districts everywhere to follow.

DIVE INTO INQUIRY
Amplify Learning and Empower Student Voice

By Trevor MacKenzie

Dive into Inquiry beautifully marries the voice and choice of inquiry with the structure and support required to optimize learning. With *Dive into Inquiry*, you'll gain an understanding of how to best support your learners as they shift from a traditional learning model into the inquiry classroom, where student agency is fostered and celebrated each and every day.

CLASSROOM MANAGEMENT IN THE DIGITAL AGE
Effective Practices for Technology-Rich Learning Spaces
By Patrick Green and Heather Dowd

Classroom Management in the Digital Age helps guide and support teachers through the new landscape of device-rich classrooms. It provides practical strategies to novice and expert educators alike who want to maximize learning and minimize distraction. Learn how to keep up with the times, while limiting time wasters and senseless screen-staring.

INNOVATE WITH IPAD
Lessons to Transform Learning in the Classroom
By Karen Lirenman and Kristen Wideen

Written by two primary teachers, *Innovate with iPad* provides a complete selection of clearly explained, engaging, open-ended lessons to change the way you use iPad in the classroom. It features downloadable task cards, student-created examples, and extension ideas to use with your students. Whether you have access to one iPad for your entire class or one for each student, these lessons will help you transform learning in your classroom.

IF I WERE A WIZARD
By Paul Hamilton

Currently, there is a global push for coding in education. Coding is the new creation tool and it gives us the ability to create new products, bring people together, and solve important problems in the world. Our youngest students learn concepts in many different ways and look for ways to connect concepts to their own lives. *If I Were a Wizard* by Paul Hamilton is designed to bridge the gap between the physical and digital and be a springboard into the magical world of coding.

THANK YOU

Thank you to the following people for allowing me to use
their ideas in my sketchnotes and to publish them in this book:

Rebecca Alber
Mark Anderson
Lee Araoz
Brian Aspinall
Kate Baker
Barbara Bray
Kathleen McClaskey
Kevin Brookhouser
Amy Burvall
Jennifer Casa-Todd
Jaime Casap
Jacques Cool
Alec Couros

George Couros
Vicki Davis
Maria Galanis
Lori Gard
David Hotler
Rushton Hurley
AJ Juliani
Alice Keeler
David Lee
Jessica Loucks
Trevor MacKenzie
Angela Maiers
Ralph Marston

Mark Martin
Peter Maxwell
Amy Mayer
Oskar Nowik
Doug Peterson
Nicolás Pino James
Jessica Sanders
Andrea Trudeau
Josh Shipp
Matthew Syed
Justin Tarte
Shelly Terrell
Richard Wells

Thank you also to the following people whose
work has appeared in my drawings:

Robert Fulgham
Taylor Mali

Karen Salmansohn
Philip Schlechty

Susan Wojcicki
Jack Zenger

A special thank you goes to
Holly Clark, Erin Casey, and the EdTechTeam Press team
for believing in this book and making it happen.